'Full of engaging character sketches and entertaining set pieces.'

Tom Gilling, *Sydney Morning Herald*

'There really is one book you should read to make you laugh, chuckle and think about what it was really like to grow up surrounded by Catholicism. Yes, Charles Waterstreet has penned the tome for you! Most nights I'd get home and couldn't put it down before smiling all the way into noddyland.'

Melissa Hoyer, *Sunday Telegraph*

'Charles Waterstreet...has tackled something very difficult—writing a childhood memoir from the perspective of a child but using the wisdom of hindsight and a more or less hybrid child/adult vocabulary—and brought it off... Waterstreet achieves a nice balance and blend of the comic and the sociological which makes the book readable and likeable...a well-written, well-organised and highly amusing book.'

Peter Corris, *Australian Financial Review*

'Everyone...who has read *Precious Bodily Fluids: A Larrikin's Memoir*, by barrister Charles Waterstreet, has come away chortling... [It] contains two characters who'll enter the pantheon of Australian literature— young Charlie's best mate "Taillight", a sort of Ginger Meggs on speed, and Albury's long-serving, legendary mayor Cleaver Bunton.'

Elizabeth Wynhausen, *The Australian*

'Charles is a country boy at heart. In his book *Precious Bodily Fluids* he brilliantly and hilariously captures the humour, tragedy and poignancy of what it was like to be a young boy growing up in rural Australia. It's an honest, vibrant account of an 11-year-old enjoying the final freedoms of his boyhood within the confines of a small Aussie country town in the early '60s.'

Leonie Dale, *Woman's Day*

'Charles Waterstreet has written a hilariously funny book. But his real achievement is historical: he's produced a true and affectionate portrait of a community which really existed and which is gone forever.'

Vaughan Tucker, *Northampton Chronicle and Echo*

'An Australian childhood memoir so warm and witty that, what with Clive James and Barry Humphries, it would appear the Ozzie male is world leader in approachable autobiographies. ... Evoking a Catholic education of the fifties and sixties, it's comic, loving, and often painfully sad: as good a biography as any Hollywood made-it. If not better.'

What's On in Birmingham

'In this hysterically funny memoir, Waterstreet relives a crazy and unforgettable part of his early life.'

Belfast Telegraph

Repeating the Leaving

an unauthorised memoir

Charles Waterstreet

AN ALISON PRESSLEY BOOK

S

SCEPTRE

A Sceptre Book

Published in Australia and New Zealand in 2001
by Hodder Headline Australia Pty Limited
(A member of the Hodder Headline Group)
Level 22, 201 Kent Street, Sydney NSW 2000
Website: www.hha.com.au

Published in association with
Belladonna Books
39 Palmer Street, Balmain NSW 2041

National Library of Australia
Cataloguing-in-Publication data:

Waterstreet, Charles.
Repeating the leaving : an unauthorised memoir.

ISBN 0 7336 1111 7.

1. Waterstreet, Charles. 2. Adolescence - Australia -
Biography. 3. Lawyers - Australia - Biography. 4. Motion
picture producers and directors - Australia - Biography.
5. Sydney (N.S.W.) - Social life and customs. I. Title.

791.430233092

Text design and typesetting by Bookhouse, Sydney
Printed in Australia by Griffin Press, Adelaide

To the men of the Order of Christian Brothers,
whose gentle nudges enabled many a young man
to negotiate the rapids of adolescence on his way
to the whirlpools and waterfalls of later life.
Their hearts were in the right place.
It was their hands you had to watch.

For the love of but not necessarily in the order of
G, P, P, V, A, J, F, R, P, M, G, C and even K

'Separation, whether physical or psychological, is a basic cause of human sadness.'

Louis Wolpert, *Malignant Sadness: The Anatomy of Depression*

CONTENTS

The Beginning
of the Beginning

'In my beginning is my end... In my end is my beginning.'

As learnt by heart from *Poems of Spirit and Action*,
Volume 2, p. 17, English syllabus,
attributed to a T. S. Eliot

There was a time I must have come to believe that God had given me the gift of speech to hide my thoughts. I don't recall when it began, but I remember exactly how it stopped.

* * *

Room three in the intensive care unit at Northside Clinic is the furthest from the glass-panelled and constantly fluoro-lit nurses' station. It is the favourite of

1

the regular suicide attemptee, many of whom suspiciously succumb to impulse at the time a vacancy occurs in room three. Its allure is what distinguishes the patient from the carer. Northside Clinic brochures highlight the circling bushland, the cosy pastoral setting and easy access to buses and trains. But very few of the self-destructive bother to read it before popping a handful of pills, dropping to their knees and putting their heads in the oven, fitting the hose over the exhaust pipe and into the car through the side window, or wandering into peak-hour traffic at a busy intersection. The regular, season-ticket patient seeks the sanctuary of room three for its outlook. If a pushy nurse pulls the heavy green daffodil-patterned curtains and off-white nets to the side, all you see is a red brick wall about three feet away (through the steel-barred window). A glimpse of gum tree or hydrangea bush would be too depressing to bear. The red brick wall is reassuring, and is as much of the world anyone in room three wants to see from the bed.

In room two lies a middle-aged police sergeant in a completely catatonic state brought about by allegations of corruption at the Police Royal Commission. His visitors enjoy the view of the grounds through his window while he stares unblinking at the ceiling. On my right in room one a beautiful farmer's wife in her late thirties from near Mudgee buzzes about in a manic mood and blue dressing gown, singing hymns and seventies pop songs. In another room a successful computer

operator prepares her hair for the next round of electro-convulsive therapy. For the first time in years, I feel
strangely at home.

Scoring room three seems out of place in my recent
wretched life. My marriage has fallen apart and my
wife has taken herself and our two-year-old son away
from Sydney to higher ground in Aspen, Colorado. My
divorce lawyer's boast of negotiating successfully for
weekend access has lowered even further my view of
my own profession. By the time I got there I'd have to
come back. Frequent flyer points would not be much
of a legacy to my son. Then suddenly our best man
apparently drowns himself in his spa pool after spending a weekend with me. Beset by financial difficulties,
I file for personal bankruptcy. Let me tell you, receiv-
ing mail addressed to The Estate of Charles Christian
Waterstreet is not cheering. It kills me before I'm dead.
My life is a country and western song.

I lose my home, but kind friends lend me a room
in their large house. I at least sleep (when I can) in my
own bed, one of a pair carefully handmade for a lover
and myself some seventeen years before. The day after
she attended my wedding—in black, I recollect: a bad
sign—my old lover began legal proceedings against me
for fraud and the return of my bed. The case came on
in the Supreme Court seventeen years after we stopped
living together. We had only lived together with our
twin beds for nearly six months. After three weeks in
court every day, facing her across the room, I could

not drag myself out of bed—whoever's—for the final day of submissions. If I lost she'd have to take it from under me. I had lost seventeen pounds. Weight loss is the only upside of major depression.

I curl in my bed for days, sweating and staring into the immediate space, like an unshelled prawn on a wet napkin. I do not want to kill myself. It would be too much effort. But I would welcome with open arms a knife-wielding madman climbing through my window.

As a barrister I have cross-examined most psychiatrists in the state over the years. There is only one that I think is worth a tinker's curse. I try to phone him for an appointment but Telecom has suspended the facility for non-payment. I walk over the Harbour Bridge to his rooms, dragging my feet like a draughthorse. They seem to have become unattached to my legs. He admits me to Northside after the same kind friends pass the hat around for a week's stay.

The only time I have ever been to a nuthouse before was to visit my mother when I was young. Now here I am, in the foetal position on the bed in room three, just like she had nearly always been while I was growing up. My three younger balding brothers envied my full head of brown hair that was just like Mum's. They inherited Dad's snooker ball hairline. But the hair doesn't travel alone and I also got the head out of which it grows. DNA, like God, works in mysterious ways.

Dr Yip is not my idea of a psychiatrist. He enters room three with a clipboard and the crispest white coat I've ever seen. He looks about twelve. He identifies himself as the Psychiatric Registrar in a language I barely understand as English. He has carefully combed black hair and black-rimmed glasses. If I wasn't so depressed I would chuckle at this Chinese Boy Wonder with the voice of a talking toy bear and his entertaining the idea of practising talking therapy. I tell him my story. He makes illegible notes on the clipboard. He tells me to lie flat on the bed.

'Close your eyes. Think of the last time you saw your mother. Consider it for a moment.'

I haven't mentioned her. He tells me to say 'I forgive you' three times. Each time, he whisks his hands over the entire length of my body from head to feet. He dusts the depression away.

I begin to see.

In the
Wet Dreamtime

If you were lucky enough to find yourself near the bitumen tennis courts, with your fingers entwined in the surrounding steel mesh, kicking the bottom netting back and forth at the magic hour, just after dusk in the spring, between the end of dinnertime and before study, while everyone else was in Chapel mumbling and growling decades of the Sorrowful Rosary, and you happened to look up at the pink and blue sky, you would see thousands of flying foxes flapping slowly and haphazardly, each pitch black, towards the flowering eucalyptus, turpentine, paperbark and banksia trees to the north of Sydney for their nightly feed.

And if one of them had looked down on this lucky boy (for flying foxes have vision twenty times stronger than ours—their retinas are folded, not flat) it might have seen the sad realisation that early spring brought to his upturned face for the first time that year, and thereafter each and every spring of the thirty-odd years that have since passed. It was almost a physical thing, sometimes a feeling as if you might reach out and touch it, this sense of pre-summer melancholy. The approach of summer was supposed to bring promise and plenty, but perhaps like everything else in this place at the bottom of the planet, it was upside down, at the arse end of the world, where the centre is rusted and everyone lives on the verandah coastline as if ready to leave. Some said it was the Irish in me, bred into my bones, in a body born many mothers and fathers ago in Clontarf, Limerick and in County Kerry, and in Thomastown, County Kilkenny, and in Cashel, County Tipperary. My bones had not yet adjusted, caught in the wrong hemisphere, and falsely believed winter was coming. April is not the cruellest month here. It's really October. All Eliot's learnt-by-heart poems would sound awkward and clumsy if he lived here.

The flying fox or fruit bat is the most Australian of mammals, lazily hanging upside down all the hot day, conserving energy, neither defying gravity nor fighting it, setting out in colonies at the first sight of darkness at speeds of up to 30 km/h, while the rest of us below trudge homeward, alone, looking at the footpath ahead.

If I were to look up now, a sharp-eyed flying fox would see a very different face, crows feet exploding like sky rockets in the skin at the sides of my eyes, the light catching the shine off the scalp under the light

7

grey dusting of hair pulled across, my brow as corrugated as a weather map, and my eyes no longer blue but as grey as a battleship cringing in my head.

As the end of 1966 approached, a life that was not above me lay ahead, outside the cast iron gates of Waverley College, permanently spreadeagled against the brick walls by chains of vines and under the great wrought iron school badge above the driveway, painted and peeling in the school colours of blue and gold with the Latin inscription in black steel letters: Virtus Sola Nobilitat—virtue alone is noble. All of us, Grantie, Simmo, The Bike and me, were repeating the leaving certificate and boarding for one reason or another. I had been considered at fifteen too young for university, the others hoped for better marks.

But what had mattered most until recently was the absolute lack of evidence of anything approaching a sexual revolution occurring within a bull's roar of the boarding school perched atop the highest point in the eastern suburbs of Sydney. My father complained that the sexual revolution came after he had run out of bullets. We were worried that it would finish before we fired off a single shot. Outside the bricks, beyond the boundaries of Birrell Street and Bronte Road, it was all happening; in our minds' eyes, guys were scoring with chicks at the drop of a hat in a hurricane. Everybody was doing it with everybody else. Except us. The papers said it was so. The *Daily Telegraph* had just run an eight-page survey of 'Sex in '66', with pictures. With flashlights under the blankets in the dormitory we passed around these pages declaring that the sexual revolution had reached Australia in Theatre, Pop Music, Films, Television, Photography, Literature, Advertising and Fashion. We were in the eye of the storm. Nothing was happening. Nothing was moving but our hands. Occasionally, reports from our former classmates at the front in university spoke of the problems of relentless promiscuity, and they wondered if they could keep it up. They claimed to yearn for a good night's sleep. The greatest danger to these teenage lovers was being run over by a beach buggy in a sandhill. They revelled in free love while we wrestled with self love.

Word of the revolution had not yet reached our sister school, Holy Cross Convent. The Little Sisters of the Rich stood at the gates with small crucifixes and holy water warding off boy messengers wearing the bright blue and gold blazers of our college. But in the third term of the year I had broken through the lines and was engaged in hand to hand combat with a real live girl. Her hand quickly on mine, whenever I approached, making incy-wincy spiders with my crawling fingers anywhere near her so-called erogenous zones or bra-strap hook. At least I was in the battle even if not in a fully-fledged fixed-bayonet charge. Grantie was miles ahead. He was dry-rooting one of the school's kitchen maids who lived in an adjoining house the Church had bought during the Depression when prices were cheap and men and women were thinking of turning Catholic for the better afterlife and needed to send their children to the right school. It was only a matter of time, Grantie said, before he'd be doing it with his pants off.

As if all of this wasn't enough, our Prime Minister, Harold Holt, up and invited Lyndon Baines Johnson, the President of the whole God damn United States of America to visit for a few days, before peace talks in Manila with other world leaders. They had become matey in July, when Holt was in Washington, and after many transPacific international telephone calls between Canberra and Washington the President finally found some time in late October. The Prime Minister had popped the right question. Such was the bond between them that it didn't seem to matter that the President was leaving his country in the middle of a congressional election while his personal domestic popularity was at an all-time low, and the Prime Minister himself would have to take time off from Federal elections to meet and greet the great man. Cynics had their say as usual. The President had had a real soft spot for us in his huge Texan heart ever since his Flying Fortress crashlanded in 1942 in Winton, Queensland, on its way to New Guinea. The soft spot was still there despite his triple bypass.

The President threw a huge party at the White House to announce his return to Australia, the first visit by a sitting President. According to reporters, his spirits were soaring, his mood sentimental, jovial and emotional.

He said, 'I love Australians. I envy all of them.' Pressmen from all over the globe were told, 'You are going to like Australians. They have a pioneer spirit.' Australians reminded him of a saying left over from frontier days in Texas. 'When you respect a man you say he's the kind of man you would pick to get behind a log with you—meaning that he has to be a man of courage and will get down with you and not run away when fired upon.' My face fired up in full blush as I read these comments in the newspaper. 'There's another Texan saying,' Johnson continued. 'He is a man you would like to go to the well with you.' This dated from Indian days, when you were just as likely to get scalped going to the well. 'I would choose an Australian to go to the well with me.'

That was us. People you could get down behind a log and go to the well with. This Johnson was one of us.

Lady Bird and his mother had given him a 16 mm movie camera during the War and he had captured his trip in 1942 as a Navy Lieutenant-Commander both in black and white and in living colour. He introduced and narrated his film at the White House theatre to engrossed reporters, describing himself as cameraman, director, producer and sometimes performer. He joked that the only similarity to a famous movie production is that its title could be *South Pacific*. The man of action had turned the camera on himself during the belly-landing of the crippled Flying Fortress near Winton. If television had been invented he could have sold the footage of the world's whackiest landing. The soundless shots of Darwin after the Jap bombing were spooky. The President-to-be must have visited a lot of hospitals because there were many shots of nurses in Melbourne, Darwin, Townsville, Port Moresby and central Queensland. One in particular seemed to be on hand everywhere.

Australian hostesses had opened their homes and hearts to GIs and made them welcome. The President had never been treated better 'except by my wife and my mother'. Lady Bird had subtitled these White House movies herself and under yet another shot of the pretty nurse she wrote: 'Why men want to get well'.

Their daughters Luci Baines and Lynda Bird were not coming. It was a pity. Lynda Bird's boyfriend, actor George Hamilton, would have loved our beaches.

On the day after the White House announcement the *Sun* had tracked down the mystery woman appearing in the President's 1942 movie. In 1966, Tessa Smallpage still kept the ex-Lieutenant-Commander's picture on her TV set, personally autographed 'With many thanks for Melbourne hospitality'. He looked like a macho Bob Hope. She had gone to Melbourne in the mid thirties to study operatic singing and during the war worked as a singer and hostess at American Servicemen's Clubs. She remembered him as being as handsome as a film star. She had met many GIs. Lyndon was her favourite. She went to America in 1947 and married another American, the vice-president of New York's Radio City Hall. As Mrs Sydney Goldman she performed at many city charity functions. She told the *Sun* that the night before she had dreamt of the President. American women love presidents who can drop their pants in the wink of an eye. American presidents love women who can drop to their knees without batting an eyelid. The British only ever go on one knee, and then only to be knighted.

The President exercised Solomon's wisdom, allocating Sydney and Melbourne exactly four hours each. There was a powerful almighty rivalry between the capital cities and even an extra minute in one city would be frowned upon by the other as favouritism. To achieve this even-handed goal the President would fly to Canberra, then to Melbourne, then back to Canberra, then to Sydney, then back to Canberra again before flying to Brisbane. He would not play favourites even if it meant spending three nights in Canberra. The President got a lot of mileage points up, keeping everybody happy. For security reasons he and his entourage would be staying at the Canberra Rex Hotel, where a special 6 feet 9 inch bed had been installed and the walls retouched with white paint where they were marked. The wife of the manager of the Canberra Rex chose yellow curtains and bedspread, which were made up by a local decorator. The Embassy strangely requested white mats for the bathroom but the management thought it would be better to have wall-to-wall nylon shag in the bathroom. The President was known to continue meetings while sitting down for a bog. The carpet would ensure a minimum of discomfort. A large colour television was to be installed, and set on Canberra's only station. His bedside radio could also pick up piped music if the mood called.

One of the reasons behind carpeting the bathroom at the Canberra Rex was to comfortably accommodate the Secret Service agents who shadowed the President wherever he went. Since Rufus W. Youngblood had thrown himself over then Vice-President Johnson a moment after President Kennedy was shot he had dogged the President's footsteps. The President didn't make a move or motion without him. G-men were sent from Washington to comb Sydney to find the safest route for the motorcade. Nothing was left to chance.

Our headmaster Old Macdonald promised that the repeating boarders could take advantage of the free public transport travel for schoolchildren and attend the City Reception at the Art Gallery.

Labor Senator Cavanagh declined the Prime Minister's invitation to the Parliamentary luncheon for the President. He would be going to an anti-Vietnam demonstration instead. He said he was afraid he would vomit if he heard the Prime Minister refer to the sacrifice for freedom in South Vietnam. 'Every piece of steak I put in my mouth would remind me of the burnt flesh from the napalm bombing in South Vietnam.'

Boy, did we live in interesting times or what?

Mum

Things are coming to a head during the repeating year. With visits to hospitals, hostels and nursing homes becoming more frequent, her stays longer and her returns home shorter, we find Mum more and more present by her absence. Dad does his best. Mum slowly drowns in the sea of herself.

During the first term holidays she is admitted to Kenmore Hospital in Goulburn under Schedule Two of the Mental Health Act. Kenmore is the last port of call for the insane or bewildered, when all else has failed. Dr Twomey writes in his referral letter: 'She has had a wide variety of psychiatric treatments at various institutions without success.' He diagnoses acute psychotic depression following repeated episodes of chronic alcoholism.

The road between Albury and Kenmore sees the two-tone EJ Holden with sheepskin covers on the front seat and Mum in the back seat jammed between her sisters, my aunts, holding her down, urging her to slow down from drinking from the flask, myself in the front passenger seat watching her in the rear vision mirror gulping down the soothing Chateau Tanunda and spilling it down her chin while an auntie grabs her hand so she doesn't inhale it. At petrol stations Dad locks the back doors and stands guard lest she make an hysterical run for it, wherever it is. I don't dare turn around to see. I watch it all in the rear vision mirror.

I'm so sorry, Charlie. I'm so sorry. He shouldn't be here.

I can't reply. I pretend I didn't hear. Invisible hands cup my ears.

Dad signs her in at Kenmore and hands over Dr Twomey's black fountain penned Referral and Scheduling Form under the Mental Health Act.

She is taken, strapped into a wheelchair, by big nurses in blue uniforms.

Her admission sheets reveal she is covered in bruises. During the three months of her admission she has ten courses of electro-convulsive therapy. Kenmore's psychiatrist Dr Tooth feels that a chronic psychotic form of depression underlies everything else and her prognosis is very doubtful. She comes home with a month's supply of Amitriptylline and a few Sparine for sleep. Dr Tooth does not think it wise to give her too many Sparine.

Mum is at home for the August holidays. The past is another country town.

Lover's Balls

Brother Moffitt's handball-hardened brick-red right fist hits the left side of my mouth like a thunder-bolt. Mr Fist, say hello to Mr Chin. The top half of my body collapses as if scissors have cut the strings holding it up but my legs lock stiff as golf sticks, leaving my head hanging like a windsock between my knees. I immediately sense I have the upper hand, although I can see two or more school chapels upside down in the distance and clouds all over the place where the school grounds should be. My whole life flashes before me. It doesn't take long. I am sixteen.

Moffitt is the size of a large outdoor lavatory with a watertank for a head. His face glows the colour of Ayers Rock. Grey-ginger hair grows out of his nostrils as if someone has shoved a pair of shaving brushes up them. But he's broken Rule Number One of the no-noes for dormitory masters at Waverley College. He has lost his temper. Done his block. Blown his stack.

Dropped his bundle. My teeny weeny little white lies that led him to it are now all but irrelevant.

As the ground shifts beneath our feet I slowly rise swan-like and shit grinning—just enough to set him off again. He'll be putty in my soft chubby hands. At last the tables are turning like a lazy susan in a cheap Chinese restaurant. I am a glutton for punishment. His black robes shake like heavy curtains in an earthquake. I wouldn't be surprised to see blood gushing out of the top of his head like a geyser. His hard, knuckled right ball of bone freezes in mid-flight, just as it's about to explode out of the black tunnel of his sleeve, on its way to me. His few remaining wits gather themselves quickly together in a scrum in that part of his head he loosely calls his brain.

The whole bloody thing arose out of a complete mis-understanding on my part. I didn't know Moffitt was watching from the Brothers Balcony when I snuck off after school, through the bushes by the front gate, down through the Charing Cross Junction for a quick pash upon the thick child-bearing lips of Georgina George behind the goalposts in the grass on the slopes of Queens Park. So when he cunningly asks me later, just before showers, where I have been all afternoon and I answer just too super-quickly Playing tennis, while making a terrifically timed sweep of a fake backhand gesture, he just loses it and whacks me from nowhere. Perhaps, on the other clenched hand, it might have been the necklace of lovebites Georgina has left just above the grimy collar of my greasetrap Penguin tennis shirt the colour of cold porridge.

Whatever it was, Brother Moffitt knows that I know that he knows that I know he has completely blown it. I play him as an intelligent ball of wool does a kitten. He orders me to stand in front of Headmaster Old Macdonald's empty office in the quadrangle while he fetches him from Father Keneally's weekly confession for the Brothers in the chapel.

Old Macdonald will be irritated as he has much to tell college chaplain Father Keneally, what with the dozing off in Sunday mass for a minute or two; the mouthed, soundless but unmistakable swearword at Brother Franklin's deadbutt to finish off the handball game; the overeating at the last feast day; not to mention the thoughts, the thoughts, the dreadful thoughts that won't go away despite his ever-increasing age. No, he wouldn't mention any of these matters to Father Keneally. It would be far too embarrassing. These brown-robed Franciscans with their white ropes for belts are much too holier than thou in these matters. He would make up an equal sin that he had not committed and suffer the punishment and take any absolution that Keneally meted out like the man he is. After all, a sin is a sin is a sin. God isn't interested in the actual details if your heart is in the right place. Surely. Surely. His innermost thoughts have a very broad brogue, and when he thinks surely surely it sounds to the alert as if he is calling out a girl's name.

When I was much younger and just fresh to the college and on the verge of disbelieving, I sought out Old Macdonald's counsel when besieged by my own evil impure thoughts. When will I ever be free from the curse of these impure thoughts? I asked him. When you are about my age, son, he answered. Seventy-one. The very next day he took me aside and softly whispered, Make that seventy-two.

In the quad I bite down on the fleshy folds of my inner cheeks as hard as I can. A thin trickle of blood from the side of my mouth would be just what the doctor ordered. I pop my upper bridge of three teeth into my pocket for further effect. My confidence grows exponentially even though it really stings trying to get some blood to flow. Moffitt will surely get what's coming to him. Maybe Old Macdonald will biff him or send him to a faraway country school or straight back to Queensland where the schools are on stilts to keep out the snakes.

It is the first time I know the thrilling upside of pain. Punishment as its own reward. I was getting it, but about to give it back plus some. To the victim go the real spoils.

I stand in front of Old Macdonald's office in my short black name-tagged nylon laddered socks in stinking Dunlop off off off white sandshoes, one without a lace, the other undone, both tongues hanging out for fresh air, my footy pants soiled from the playing paddocks of the King's School, Shore College, Scots College and this very arvo Waverley's own Queens Park, on the grassy slope beyond the goalposts. Despite the jarring ache in my jaw, despite the self-inflicted sting in my cheeks, my mood soars in anticipation.

It isn't just thinking about Georgina's plump pink puckered lips sucking the blood to the surface of my neck like a feeding fish around a pylon. Somewhere between holding hands and sinking the sausage, your average chick wants to leave her mark on you, like a dog with a tree. It gets so wild you want to do the same, and by the end of the day you both look like you've been attacked by very tall leeches. It's a teenage thing. You don't see old people in their twenties and thirties parading around with lovebites. There's no doubt about it. Georgina is part vamp, part vampire, but way past virgin. I button the top of my shirt and unfold the collar as high as it will go while pulling my head into my sloping beer-bottle shoulders. These bloodshot little moons orbiting my neck had been red rags to that bull Moffitt.

It isn't even the tummy-tickling prospect that some day soon Georgina and I will again be playing thrill-necked lizards with each other. No sirree, mister. The greatest thing about the whole afternoon, better than the red welts themselves, will be the telling and retelling of it to my mates.

We lap up this kind of stuff. This whole repeating year, Grantie, Simmo, The Bike and me had stuck to each other like Tarzan's Grip. Bed by bed at night in the dorm, desk by desk during the day, and towel by towel on every second Sunday at Bronte Beach. We gagged and giggled a lot, especially when it was supposed to be semi-serious. Like when I had my first date with Georgina after school and we were kissing in the laneway and I was holding her head in both hands, with its Prince Valiant helmet of blue-black hair. I couldn't wait to get away, after a while, to tell the boys what I had done. This was at the same time that I was actually doing it.

But even then we tended to exaggerate things a little, and after we had unlocked our lips and I had high-tailed it back to school, I gave myself a little lovebite on my upper arm. I had to. It wasn't enough just to keep up with each other. We had to top each other. It's hers, I claimed. Bullshit, said Simmo. They held me down and The Bike made me spit out my bridge into his hand. He took an impression of my teeth with his chewing gum. It matched the bite on my arm perfectly. The Bike has a cruel spoke to him.

Nobody this year has ever topped Simmo the time he came back to school after a long weekend leave. He played it as cool as a cucumber. Didn't say a thing. When we were all undressing for bed in the locker room, he dallied just for a moment after he took his shirt off. He had blood-red lovebites all over his chest, as if each nipple had been used for target practice. He waved us away with an It's nothing. Grantie traced the bites down his chest and we goaded Simmo into pulling off his pants and showing us the rest. There were lovebites on his bum, both cheeks, and all over the upper reaches of his inner thighs. She must have been at it all weekend, said The Bike. I reckoned he'd need a blood transfusion. There must have been more than one girl involved. Simmo said there were, and he'd just lain down on the bed like a sow with a litter. Simmo was no oil painting in the looks department but there was something about him you couldn't exactly put your finger on and girls insisted on putting their mouths there. Whatever it was, he had it in spades, hearts, clubs and diamonds. He took off all his clothes and twisted slowly around on his tiptoes as if Jesus Christ himself was a toyshop ballerina while we carefully examined his many stigmata. As he turned, he seemed to levitate ever so slightly, while we murmured amongst ourselves, looking to see who did what and where. It was The Bike who first noticed the clean circle that each bite had. He put his black Buddy Holly glasses on top of his head and took a close look. We had our fingers extended like multiple St Thomases at each impression, wondrous at these tiny miracles, when The Bike announced at the top of his voice These are frauds, downright frauds! They were done by a vacuum cleaner, probably an Electrolux, the round edges are a complete giveaway. Simmo fell quickly to the ground. Gotcha. Gotcha. Gotcha bad. And he had. Simmo was still a pantsman even though his lovebites were self-inflicted. He could have done the real thing but he was up to his elbows with the vacuum cleaner all weekend. We once called him Lover Boy. Now he was Hoover Boy. There followed copycat crimes. A rash of day boys escaping at home to the secrecy of the broom closet with Mum's vacuum cleaner. Brother Moffitt thought it was the German measles. Old Macdonald knew better. He could spot self-abuse within an arm's length of himself, in fading light, with his eyes tightly closed.

* * *

Old Macdonald and Moffitt still haven't shown up so I begin thinking up the best way to present the incident to Simmo and the boys, with all its slow motion ducks and weaves, my tricky footwork, the bloodletting from my mouth by Moffitt and the bloodsucking from my neck by Georgina. The story nearly always is better than the thing itself. Boy oh boy, would I have a ball with this—and it isn't even over yet.

Things have really started falling into place since the third term began. Georgina told her best friend Katie Hall that she liked me, and Katie told Mick Mullen, who was the First Fifteen captain, who told Billy Marshall at inside centre, who told Cranky O'Brien at halfback, who was mightily pissed off because he was going out with Georgina at the time. He exploded. Eventually someone told me, and before you knew it within three months I had a date with her and Cranky O'Brien was sidelined from the Georgina George game.

The excitement of this arvo's events rises up slowly from the ground into the balls of my feet and creeps on all fours up my legs. At first it's just a jig, moving the weight from one foot to the other. Before long my legs are infected with it and I am jogging up and down on the spot outside Old Macdonald's office. Oh oh. Here it comes, like the Blowhole of Kiama. The simultaneous and urgent urge to pee and poop that precedes all great occasions like the showing of the Saturday night movie in the Great Hall, the feel of a signed weekend leave pass in Old Macdonald's spidery scrawl in your hand, or the sight of the dining hall on the Boarders Annual Feast Day, when you burst out first from chapel and no one has sat down and the food and cakes and lollies are set out on white plates with opened bottles of soft drinks in the middle of each table surrounded by silver paper and crackerjacks and coloured crepe paper party hats with spikes for crowns.

I clench down hard front and back, tight as a fist inside, checking my jogging to something like the motion in Olympic walking competitions. The big hand of inner excitement grips my heart and starts banging it against my chest so hard I think it might break open like fibro. Soon it is in my head, making me giddy in its thrall. And all of this going on in me because I can't wait to crow about it to Simmo and the boys. Necking the afternoon away with Miss Georgina George, getting punched square in the chin with Moffitt's best shot and not crying about it or saying a word. The bragging to come. But if the truth be known I don't feel like a real hero at all. Sure, I'd show the war wounds around my throat to all and sundry after dinner and wear them for days like medals won in the battle of the sexes, but I am really like a soldier returning home from the front with an eye-patch to a hero's welcome, having had his eye poked out by a careless pool player in the mess hall.

* * *

There's a condition that you won't find written up in *Pix*, *Post*, *Playboy* or even *Man Junior*. Not even in the new Wyndham Scheme biology books which Trevor Trudgeon takes to the toilet to jerk off on is there anything noted about this troubling condition, or in The Bike's parents' medical books on the reproductive system. But it's as real as acne or growing pains. (Nobody believed me when I had growing pains in my shins, and in my knees, and in my thighs. The pain was so intense I yearned to be a dwarf when I grew up. Dad said I'd grow out of it. My Nana said it was all in the head. I wished I'd got growing pains in my willie. It was too small for my liking.)

It hits you somewhere between fifteen and seventeen, somewhere between petting and poking, and right between your big toes, but higher. Lover's balls. It's the curse of the kissing class. Simmo said it was caused by endolphins which sound like some sort of fish sperm.

Apparently we all emit these endolphins, and if a chick's endolphins get up your nose and into your bloodstream the overexposure leads to this dull but painful ache in your groin that leaves you all bent over in pain. Grantie doesn't get it because he's dry-rooting already. Lover's balls is growing pains in transit.

It's unlike anything you've ever felt before. At first I mistook it for Mrs Westie's cooking. But it was below the pit of my stomach and above my bum. My first brush with the pain that dare not speak its name was doing endless Prides of Erins at dance classes on Sunday nights at St Pat's Hall. The cream of Albury's latest Young Catholic crop circling around Mrs Fitzpatrick who in white gloves clapped in the centre to the strains of Reg Kidney and his Teatime Five on the stage. Blue nosed endolphins plunged through the sweat and dangling streamers and into our own noses. St Pat's Hall filled with the scent of splashes of 4711 and Rexona roll-on and the white haze of Johnson and Johnson's baby powder. To the tapping toes of Mrs Fitzpatrick's dancing pumps, to the strings and electric accordion of Reg Kidney, and passing from handkerchiefed hand to handkerchiefed hand of the Belles of the Riverina, I learnt the steps of the Pride of Erin and the intense inner pain of lover's balls.

The afternoon pash session with Georgina is catching up with me. Fast. It hits me like a sudden knee in the groin. There is only one cure, and that's impossible in the quadrangle in front of the whole school.

Lover's balls happens when your sperm turns toxic. It backs up from your cock and overflows like a blocked cistern into the area above your balls. God gave us the condition and the cure in our hands. Girls are so lucky they don't get lover's balls. I guess periods are part and parcel of His even-handed approach.

I am falling apart in the quadrangle. Piece by painful piece.

* * *

Moffitt and me have been allergic to each other from the get go. He's been gunning for me ever since he arrived from Gregory Terrace Unchristian Brothers school near Brisbane with a powder keg personality and pale blue eyes that would've unsettled a blind man. He measured me up earlier in the year under his albino eyelashes and found me wanting. Moffitt saw straight through me. The fact that I hardly did any work and I was Dux of the College really got up his bristly nose. It was a repeating year after all. He would come up behind me in the yard and meander past while I almost hunched in fear and he'd look dead at me and say I know your game, Waterstreet. Shit. I'd wish he'd tell me because frankly I had no game plan that I was aware of. Tell me, I thought. For God's sake. He rags Simmo, Grantie and The Bike as well. We're the opposite of teacher's pets. We're teacher's hated wild animals.

The fact that the seams of his black surplice come

apart at the shoulders across his immense back when he flexes scares the living daylights out of me. All year he's exuded a brooding menace, and finally with three weeks to go he's exploded. So inside, deep in my stomach, is this overwhelming fist of fear. It isn't the leather strap I fear. Repeating boarders' hands are out of bounds and the reach of the likes of Moffitt. The Brothers are very even-handed. When they give you six it's three on the left and three on the right. We're too old for that. We are sixteen, some seventeen. No, I'm just plain old scared of him. The only thing that keeps me from doing a runner from the quadrangle is thinking about whether to tell the boys I hit him back with a lightning left or a right-hand cross.

The storm may pass over but the story will stay. The stuff of our lives is the collecting of stories, but only the lonely tell their stories to themselves. It doesn't matter if you fudge a little, add a smart alec remark here and there, make someone else the butt of the joke, redraw the line in the sand outside the playpen, as long as you lay them in the aisles and keep them laughing. Everybody knows nothing is really true. I mean really and truly true. Not even what you see with your own eyes. But what counts in the end is how you tell it.

I think I'm really good, but Simmo is the master. I need some seed of truth, some event, something. He starts with nothing, zero, from scratch, and makes the whole thing more believable than real life itself. Moffitt's cracker punch will give me the makings of a yarn to shake Simmo's tree. I have to get the blood coming out of my mouth. Shit, even if it doesn't, I'll tell them it did. It's the same thing in the end.

A couple of dozen junior boys in straw boaters are gawking down from all three sides of the upper floors of the joined buildings that together make what is called a quadrangle for some strange reason. Maths is not the school's strong suit. The rumble of pre-shower play from the bathrooms is louder than normal. Everyone is excited because immediately after dinner and rosary in the chapel we are all to board the three waiting blue-yellow school buses in Salisbury Road and be shipped in convoy and in uniform to the Town Hall for Speech Night.

Copping one of Moffitt's hammerhead hands flush on my chin was not what I'd had in mind when I blinked my blue eyes open that morning when Brother Mein Furner clapped his little white stubby but loud hands over his head and in the boys' ears while walking up and down the spaces between the beds in the dormitory like a small Spanish flamenco dancer in a black habit. I'd been thinking about the man who has a direct line to the Vatican, which has a direct line to God, waiting to present me with the treasured Reverend Brother L. B. Tevlin Memorial Prize for Dux of College. His Eminence Cardinal Gilroy, the man himself, lovingly called by Catholics the Old Cheese because of the permanently frozen smile, who will be officiating on the dais on the stage under the great organ at the Town

Hall. My Aunt Faith says he looks so divine in red. Mum is coming by the Daylight Express from Albury to bear witness to my kissing Old Cheese's ring. It's not as bad as it sounds. Lucky prize-winners have to kneel on one knee before His Grace Old Cheese and pash the purple ring on his middle finger. Without tongue, said Simmo, his own firmly planted in his cheek.

Now what sort of fine mess have I gotten myself into this time, Stan? I lean my head right back, until my illegally long hair touches between the blades of my back. I can see the little faces of the young boarders on the second floor, leaning out of the brickwork like flowers growing straight out of concrete. It takes me a moment to realise that they are not blowing me kisses but about to rain mouthfuls of spittle down. Little Curtis gets me smack bang in the forehead. Kids today give you no respect.

I backstep into Old Macdonald's office door jamb, pushing tight against the door until I nearly merge with wood, out of spit's way. In no time at all the bitumen is peppered with long and short bursts of spitfire sprinkling down like a summer shower that can't make up its mind. I push my upturned palm out like a hopeful farmer only to cop a huge gob which I grip tightly as I shake a furious fist at those above. I wipe my palm on the front of my shirt, where it blends nicely.

Time is ticking away. Steam billows out from all four shower blocks of the old building and wafts up and under the white plaster statue of Our Lady of the Mount. Every day during school term at about this time Our Lady of the Mount gets a lovely steam bath, but miraculously her weight and complexion never change. Hands together and eyes to Heaven, Our Lady of the Mount has perched atop the old school building for over forty years daring, just daring, the lightning to strike. From her domain on the highest point in the Eastern Suburbs she can see from Circular Quay to the Heads and way out to sea. The Catholics have always got the best positions. There were more than a few of us in the First Fleet and the Great Irish Famine kicked the numbers along. The Sisters Without Mercy own half the foreshore at Rose Bay and the Little Sisters of the Rich claim the better locations on the North Shore. It's a pity the Church doesn't pass it around a bit more. Our Lady of the Mount doesn't bat a concrete eyelid during the most ferocious storms. Hailstones bounce off her head like ping pong balls. My favourite teacher, if there is such a thing, is Brother McGrath. He claims Our Lady of the Mount's survival is proof, proof positive, that there is a God in Heaven. It's a miracle, he proclaims with open arms. He loves to gesticulate. There's a whiff of wog on his mother's side. We have him for English this year. He stands up the front of the class with a poetry book opened at *The Rime of the Ancient Mariner* in one hand and with the other points to himself and says I am the water and then, pointing around the class, cries You are the sponge. Everyone in class pipes up You are the water and we are the sponge, like in the Litany, and we all break up laughing, Brother McGrath as well. He's real cool. If it weren't for the black togs he'd pass for human.

All the hot water must be finished by now and I'll have to count to ten and run back and forth under the cold water, my skin turning blue and my willie disappearing into pubic hair. Moffitt must be giving Old Macdonald the long version. With any sort of luck the lovebites will fade if they take any longer. I can't feel any lumps with the tips of my fingers. Those Greek girls are mightily passionate, making gooey noises all the time, but beware of Greeks bearing gifts. Georgina has left me with the worst case of lover's balls.

Georgina George's father is your full-on Zorba the Greek. Couple of bottles of retsina and he has the hankie out and is dancing like he's having a crap at the same time. I reckon all the breaking of plates after meals is just a clever way of ducking the washing up. A guy could make a fortune selling paper plates in Greece. He's a doctor and has shortened his name by lopping off a couple of dozen vowels and consonants. He must have been exhausted because choosing the name Georgina can't have taken a huge effort. It was a lucky thing they didn't have a son. George George. Imagine Moffitt asking for his surname. George, sir. Listen to me, sonny, I asked for your surname. George, sir. Don't get smart with me. It's George, sir. Biff. Wham. And back to Dad for some treatment.

Georgina's mum is not Greek and it really doesn't matter what else she was because in the Greek community you're either Greek or nothing. I am less than nothing in Doctor George's eyes. He has nothing to worry about. Yet. Georgina has delicious pale breasts the size of small planets but every time I put my hand anywhere near them she moves it like a chess piece. If my hand wasn't attached to my arm so tightly it would end up over the Harbour Bridge in North Sydney somewhere. She usually only dates someone in the back line of the First Fifteen. Simmo says she swapped airheads for eggheads. I am second row forward in the Sevenths. That's right, I explained to Dad. The Sevenths. He didn't think the school was that big.

I can hear the clinking of plates and tinkling of cutlery in the dining room. The chef will be opening the big cans of dog food that pass as stew when boiled in water. I never thought I'd miss Mrs Westie's burnt-to-a-crisp haricot chops. The college kitchens exude an unusual aroma that suppresses appetite. I think Mein Furner invented it in Science Class to save school overheads. I haven't the heart to tell Dad how bad it is, with him working day and night behind the bar and Mum mostly in hospital and four other kids waiting in the wings for boarding school. The Brothers are robbing him blind, one hundred dollars a term and shoving forty of us in a dormitory and serving dog food in its own gravy. If it wasn't for the slice of white bread we'd wither on the vine. The First Fifteen boarders get steak for breakfast on Saturdays during the season while the rest of us count how many baked beans there are in the bowl. The Bike cried out for fried fresh fish for brain food when we were sitting for the outside exams. Pig's bottom said the Brothers. That'll do I said, it must be better than this.

The sun is going down behind Our Lady of the Mount and the four great metal arches on which she stands cast a weird tangle of shadows across the quadrangle. The cool makes me instinctively rub my hands together, reminding me to clip young Curtis over the ear later.

Moffitt disappeared into the passageway leading to the chapel but I keep a keen eye on the new building to my left in case of a sneak attack. These banana-benders have no morals when it comes to discipline. They love the sound of leather on the young skin of errant boys, especially if it accidentally hits the inside of the wrist. Simmo says he hates us because we refuse to cower, but the waiting is bringing out the coward in me. Old Macdonald had grabbed the best office for himself in the new building, which he almost built single-handedly from the ground up. The old school had been bursting to the rafters with pupils because the Pope refused to allow birth control and Catholic couples were breeding like rabbits. So Old Macdonald started a huge fundraising scheme to finance a new wing or two at the school. We called it the Shit-a-Brick Fund, but it was really Give-a-Brick and the Brothers pumped out the pleading letters from the Gestetner until the guilts got everyone buying a brick for a dollar. Old Cheese himself opened the new building and the great unsung rock and roller Johnny O'Keefe turned up in black Ray-Bans and nodded off during the speeches. We all peered down from the balconies onto the crowd of dignitaries wondering whether any others would nod off during Old Macdonald's welcoming speech.

Moffitt springs out of the shadows armed with Old Macdonald at his side. If I believed in Our Lady of the Mount I would whisper a little prayer out of the side of my mouth as I am still biting down on the inner cheeks. Moffitt is striding ahead a step or two in his anxiety to get at me and Old Macdonald has to skip as best he can to keep up. The hard crunch of the Brothers' boots on the gravel passageway echoes through the quadrangle like a distant drumroll. I spit on the ground in front of me to see if there is any blood but I can't tell which blob is mine among the spatters. I resist the urge to rush out and meet them halfway by trying to back through the wooden door. The sunset behind them makes Moffitt look like a huge black building with two small blue windows and Old Macdonald a gigantic lean-to. Boarders are rushing out of the shower block with wet hair and in towels to take a peek. The smell of blood is in the air but there is no sign of it yet on my chin.

Moffitt growls for me to explain myself to the

Headmaster. I have pulled my head in so far that my neck looks like the side of a piano accordion. I try to speak. Nothing comes out. Moffitt is given to the use of army language. He was an adjutant in the cadets. He prefers saluting to blessing himself. Sometimes in chapel his mind wanders off to battle and he pulls himself together with a clicking of the heels and a half salute that turns into a high-handed signing the cross. He tells Old Macdonald I was AWOL this afternoon. To make matters worse, I'd straight out lied to his face about it. He reckons I was plain insubordinate.

Old Macdonald has seen it all. He's seen them come and go. He knows he isn't hearing it all. In fact, he's hardly hearing it at all, and he pulls out his little red transistor hearing aid and turns it up to full volume. He must have had it off during confession, hoping to avoid his sentencing. He is startled at first at the sound it makes. Like most old men he has ears the size of serving plates holding his thin wire spectacles firmly in place. He's about half as big as Moffitt but twice the size inside. His skin is the colour of cauliflower but as smooth as a grandmother's. He walks like Robbie the Robot, feet never leaving the ground, with a slight lean towards an imaginary headwind. He peers at me while Moffitt rants and raves into his earpiece. Wrinkles gather like the tops of curtains along his soft purple lips and criss-cross his face as if drawn haphazardly by a child. He opens his mouth and says something. I can't hear it. He speaks so quietly that the words go into freefall as soon as they hit the air. You'd have to cup your ear under his chin to catch what he is saying. Sorry? I say, hoping he'll repeat himself. Instead he misunderstands and says something that sounds like Enough said, get on up and have your shower. But I can't be sure because Moffitt starts going on about my neck, pulling down my collar with his huge fist, with me pulling away and scrunching up my shoulders. Show the Headmaster! he demands. How do you explain that? Old Macdonald looks on while the tug of war with the top of my shirt continues. Explain that! Tennis ball, sir. Moffitt turns terracotta. And the others? Tennis balls, sir.

I forget to duck.

The rest is, as they say, history—a subject divided into Ancient and Modern at Waverley College, leaving a couple of hundred years in the middle untouched except by Religious Knowledge.

I catch the last shower just as it turns luke-cold. Our Lady of the Mount smiles concretely over the quadrangle, dreaming of being alabaster marble one day after the new building is paid off.

Speech Night

The hickeys glow like red-hot coals in the long mirror that divides the handbasins of the third floor dormitories' shower facilities from each other. We repeaters have Mein Furner to watch over us, and he does so with a special enthusiasm during showers as he patrols up and down, hands behind his back like Prince Philip, ready to pounce on slippery soap with sleeves pulled up and hand it over with a crooked smile. We know he has crushes on the footy players among us, and although I am clad only in a Waterstreets Hotel embroidered towel that feels like a hessian bag he is nowhere to be seen when I drop the soap. It's enough to give a bloke an inferiority complex. I'm sure I'm scarred for life, being the object of indifference for Furner's footy player fetish.

Simmo comes out of the locker room in his bright blue blazer and sandy brown hair all Brylcreemed into a snow cone on its head, coming out of his forehead like a unicorn's horn. What kept you, Charlie? I thought I might have to accept your prize tonight in absentia. Where's that, mate? Simmo's a whiz at the Latin and you have to be on your toes around him. He is getting the Latin prize—the Reverend Brother E.C. Fields Memorial Prize donated by Mr and Mrs G. Bussel— tonight. I hope I don't have to follow you to Old Cheese's ring, I say, I hate the taste of Brylcreem.

Jesus H. Christ! he bellows when he spies the blood-shot sputniks I'm admiring in the mirror. Someone described Simmo as having a face like a twisted sand-shoe, but Simmo said that was a bit unfair to the sandshoe. What he lacks in looks he makes up for in other departments. He claims to speak fluent Latin and to give excellent French. We can't confirm either, but he has personality to burn. He has more wisecracks than a nunnery. He's a born storyteller, but he has the kind of face even a mother wouldn't love, unless of course he's taken after her side of the family. Everything is pretty normal until you get to just past the eyes, where it all seems to cave in to the biropoint of his jaw like a sandhole in the desert. He speaks out of a mouth the size of an inny belly button, but he speaks better than an encyclopedia salesman. He has the gift despite a very small gab.

Grantie, on the other hand, is often asked by bar-bers whether he minds if they take his photo to put in their front window. Like the merinos on his family's farm near Dubbo, he has been bred for the stud market.

His whole head looks capped. He loves a joke as much as the better guy, but the problem is he can't remember them, so he writes them down in a small spiral notebook in tiny pencilled longhand, numbered in order of laughs raised. My Aunt Faith would say he was left behind the door when they were handing out brains, but when you look that good the rest is just baggage. He gets along fine. He is repeating the leaving in the vain expectation that they might add last year's marks to this year's to get him a pass. Girls love him—at least until they find he's made notes to guide their conversation on dates. His ad libs are the best rehearsed in town.

By now Simmo and Grantie are on either side of me, running their fingers over the lovebites and suggesting disguises. Wear the tie above the collar, says Grantie. Simmo looks at him but realises that Grantie thought irony was Australian for iron, like brekkie, sunnies, mozzies, blowies. Grantie clicks his fingers and rushes back into the locker room, emerging in seconds with a tube of Clearasil. This'll do the trick, he says, and dabs it on the infected areas. I rub it in and it works a treat, except I look like Craters Craddock, the boy with the worst acne in school. They buzz off to the dining room and I go quickly to the locker room to change. It smells of damp and Dencorub.

The Bike is last as usual. He'd be late for his own funeral. His tight wavy hair looks like it was Gladwrapped, with his oval face hiding behind Buddy

41

Holly glasses. You wouldn't know he was a real rabble-rouser by the look of him. I notice that when The Bike's eyeballs bulge from their sockets ever so slightly, they push out like cocktail onions from a martini drinker's mouth. His family of doctors lives three streets away and decided this year that boarding might bring some discipline to his life. Little do they know. His mother is a specialist in women's plumbing and his father in men's. He is an only child and spoilt by the many nannies who raised him while his parents worked. He keeps a pushbike in the hedge near the front gate and unbeknownst to the lazy school gardener makes it home most afternoons and raids the pantry for emergency supplies for the starving repeating boarders. Simmo gave him the nickname and it has stuck to such an extent that most boys don't know his real name. Even the Brothers call him The Bike, without any idea of its origin. What a hoot it all is.

My locker is jam-packed with smelly clothes, and I have to borrow one of The Bike's shirts he collected this afternoon. Dad used the very same locker room when he boarded, and Old Macdonald even taught him. A lot of history is scratched into these cedar lockers, mainly with the points of penknives. Some etchings date back before the War. Crudely drawn hearts encircle long-lost initials of lovers. Simmo's handwritten addition with the point of a compass is Brother Furner loves Littlemore, the fair-haired teacher's pet in the fifth form dorm. He's always helping him with his homework.

My laundry works on the principle that once I've worn everything I start again from the bottom of the pile in my locker, which I reason must have self-cleaned itself by then. The Bike's shirt is three sizes too small but will have to do. It's lucky that Dad isn't coming tonight because last time we spoke, when I rang reverse charge to Albury, he asked me about all these shirts I was buying on his David Jones account and how come they were all different sizes. I had to mimic interference into the mouthpiece and tell him Old Macdonald was calling for me and hang up quickly. He'd be ropable if he knew I was getting the shirts on his account and selling them half-price to day boys. Fathers tend not to understand the free enterprise system nowadays.

This last year of school has found me a little tubby. Stealing a leaf out of Dad's book, I tell people I'm big-boned. I can't work out where all the weight is coming from because they only serve the usual small portions of dog food at school. You couldn't feed a chihuahua on it. Somehow the school photo of the Sevenths shows me with Siamese thighs, joined all the way from the knees to the groin. The threat of congenital thyroid iodine deficiency shows in the beefeater chins forming under my nose. I am turning into my parents, with Mum's eyes and Dad's chins. Tuckshop arms flap like saddle bags and the lame explanation of puppy fat is wearing thin.

The Bike bulges muscles like a balloon animal, which he seems to have acquired without any effort at all. His parents probably shot him up with something. Big night, eh? as he claps a hand around behind me while I run a couple of fingers through wet hair on the way to the dining room. You could shave off the shine on the school suit I wear. If you shaved. My shoes haven't seen Kiwi since Mum bought them from Mates. The broken laces barely twist through two holes and I've pulled my socks inside out, which means they, like the underwear, will be good for another week.

One of a repeater's life's rewards is a dining room table as far from the Brothers' tables as is possible in a dining hall holding over two hundred and built for fifty. The Brothers are cashing in on the baby boomer boarders. The Brothers' tables are closest to the kitchen so that their steaks and fries, their Neopolitan ice-cream and fresh fruit salad with cherries straight out of the can, and their cups of endless tea, get to them as quickly as the kitchen help's legs and trolleys can carry them. By the time our dog food gets to the repeaters' table it's piping cold and curdled. It is always inedible, but in varying degrees of inedibleness. Again it's a scam by the Brothers, who serve up the dog food and then cash in again at the tuck shop after dinner, where Smith's Crisps, Twisties and Violet Crumbles are sold at top corner store prices.

The junior boarders sit in tables of eight closest to the Brothers so that the latter can keep a sharp eye and a loose hand on them. Mein Furner keeps a special eye out for Littlemore. Brother Toohey claps hands to call for disgrace before meals and leads us off. Bless us this day for this thy dog food which we are about to throw up.

The four of us sit together with another four repeaters and recite the prayer together, except for Grady who still believes in all that religious junk. If his nose bleeds he thinks it's some sort of stigmata.

The cutlery are real museum pieces. Most of the knives have broken bone handles and look like they were found on an anthropological dig in the middle of Australia. The forks have prongs going in all directions but parallel. The spoons are leftovers from a Uri Geller dinner party. The so-called stew is so thin on the meat that a vegetarian with a strong stomach could eat it in good conscience. But tonight's alleged meal isn't much of a concern to anyone at our table because we plan to feast on hamburgers with the works at the Greek café near the Town Hall. Our whole lives revolve around our tummies and our tummy bananas. That's what the Brothers call them during what passes for sex education talks. It seems the information is coming from us to them. They are the ones who need the education. We need the sex.

The Brothers really hate it if you leave your plate with food on it, so we all scrape ours onto Grady's plate. He eats it all up like he's doing penance. I say I'm glad I'm not sleeping in the bed next to Grady's tonight. When he opens his bedclothes in the morning it's like a gas attack in the trenches in World War I. Nearby boarders slowly fall down next to their beds in a swoon. There aren't many ways a cook can ruin jelly but at Waverley College they have perfected the art of making jelly a liquid every time. Grady gulps it up. He could have all the jelly through a straw.

Being the oldest boys at school allows us to leave the table before the others. It's to allow us to get to study earlier. But it's a real farce. We stand and push our chairs under the table and bend our heads down, pretend to mumble disgrace after meals and then do a devil's circle touching our left and right shoulders and forehead. The only thanks we're giving are for nothing. Please God don't let me throw up.

Grantie reckons he spends 99 per cent of his time thinking about sex and the other 7 per cent on food. There's little chance he'll get the Rotary Bondi Junction prize for mathematics tonight.

The four of us are thick as thieves but there's one thing they do that I hate. I just go along for the company. We head down to the day boys' toilet block where there is one solitary cubicle that has a door. The Brothers have taken all the doors from the toilets in the boarders' block so that you can't have a crap without someone perving at you. It is a pathetic attempt to stop us wanking during the day. They'll have to get up a bit earlier than that to stop us. That's why God invented holes in our pockets. So we can get off quickly during class.

The four of us cram into the corner crapper which usually has a couple of floaties bumping into unsinkable cigarette butts. Even when you pull the chain nothing happens and the stink is even worse than the dog food. The Bike pulls a box of brand new Menthol Alpines from one sock and some Redhead matches from the other. Simmo, Grantie and The Bike take a cigarette each, sniffing the length under their noses like wine buffs, while I keep up my end by lighting them up.

I hate fags, probably because I've been force-fed fumes all my life in the pub and from my parents. I light up The Bike's first because they're his treat and he sucks it in, the end glowing bright red in the dim light. With the same match burning I hold out my hand to Grantie. When he's lit up I flick the match into the dunny. Captain Jack Saunders (retired) has taught me that it's bad luck to light three cigarettes from one match. The Hun could line up a shot at you in your bunker by the third light. Although there isn't room for a dwarf in the toilet, let alone a Hun with a gun, I've always been superstitious. Avoiding stepping on cracks in the school quadrangle bitumen requires you to walk like Rudolph Nureyev. One school of thought is that if you step on a crack you break the devil's back. But I've left all that religious nonsense behind. I avoid stepping on cracks, walking under ladders and crossing the track of a black cat. With superstitions you never know if they are true because you dare not test them. Religion you know is just crap. There's a whole world of difference between believing in superstitions and believing in God.

When I strike a new match, Simmo holds my hand and brings it near to his mouth. With his greased-up snow cone of hair there's a chance he'll catch fire if you aren't careful.

So they all puff away while I inhale their smoke, and we tell jokes in the foggy corner cubicle and laugh and giggle until we hear the coughing and spluttering of the school buses starting up. We wave the air with our hands and eventually it clears enough so we can see each other, and we rush out to get the prize seats at the back of the bus.

* * *

Catholics are steeped in tradition. At Waverley we are steeper than Everest in traditions. Speech Night at the Town Hall is so special an occasion that the Brothers send their habits out for dry cleaning to get the year's chalk out, so they'll look their black best on the stage behind Old Cheese, who in his purple robes looks more like blue vein cheese. Speech Night is aptly named. It isn't Silent Night. The prize-giving is just an excuse for every Brother, priest, bishop and cardinal on the payroll to get up on the podium and tell the parents what a bargain they are getting for their money at Waverley. I wish I could tape their speeches because I'd like to have a copy for those nights when I toss and turn in bed and can't get to sleep. After a couple of minutes of Old Macdonald or Old Cheese I'd be in such a deep sleep that even Mandrake the Magician's loudest click wouldn't wake me.

As the bus rattles down Oxford Street we keep an eye out for chicks on the footpaths. When we see a cutie we all stick our tongues onto the back window and drool. The saliva runs down like rain. Most chicks turn their heads away in disgust, with a quick hand over the side of their face. The occasional one pokes her tongue out back at us. Grantie says they're goers for sure. But it would be impossible to tell Brother Marshall to stop the bus so we could pick them up. But we make mental notes of the shops they are in front of so we can cruise by some Saturday when we have more time and freedom on our hands.

Along Oxford Street there are American and Australian flags on every telegraph pole, on every tree, on every light pole. Across Taylor Square the large painted banner proclaims Sydney Goes Gay for LBJ. Posters are in shop windows with pictures of President Johnson, saying All the way with LBJ. It is incredible to think that we are in a bus that is actually travelling along a road that will soon be used by a limousine that contains the President of the United States. It sends a shiver down your spine.

* * *

I catch a glimpse of myself in the rear vision mirror of the bus as I exit at the Town Hall steps and I have to admit that I cut a pretty cool picture. The Bike's shirt is so small it makes my body look like a bulging sportsman's. The Clearasil has rubbed off onto the top of the collar, and my hair bristles out of my old broken straw boater like thick weeds.

We run up the steps into the Town Hall under a huge LBJ banner with his photograph the size of a house and printing exclaiming Welcome President Johnson.

The auditorium is chock-a-block with mums, dads and assorted children. Mum was supposed to come but she's a notorious no-show. It isn't her fault, and I half hope she won't be there, because you never know. It's better to expect nothing, then you'll never be let down and it will all be a pleasant surprise. So I always expect the worst, and most times I'm right. I can't see her head among the ladies' black felt box hats with lace and odd feathers. Catholic women have to wear a hat in church but men have to be bareheaded. I suppose it's to stop the priest being tempted. But we reckon most are queer anyway and it's the men who need head protection. Waverley mothers know the Town Hall is not a church, but with Old Cheese there it might be a sort of temporary cathedral. So most wear hats, and even look left and right for the blessing bowls when they enter.

The most interesting part of the whole evening will be to see whose sister has turned up and try to catch a seat near them. Old Boys of the college gather in groups in the foyer and tell each other how well they look and how little they've changed, and try as hard as hell to remember each other's names. Kids run up and down on the marble floor, just for the sake and sound of it.

The loudspeaker system crackles to life and everyone takes their places as if called to attention. Simmo and I sit together next to some folks we don't know. I run the front of my shoes down the back of the opposite leg of my trousers to get up a shine in anticipation. We have the very best seats in the house. Back row.

Old Macdonald starts off with prayers and the usual bullshit. The school badge and banner are draped over the giant pipes of the organ. The Brothers and lay teachers sit in rows of seats on the stage, looking out over the rest of us. Old Cheese has a huge chair right in the middle, like a king's. A choir of primary boys sings Faith of Our Fathers and Hail Queen of Heaven. The woman next to me smells like she's been swimming in a vat of 4711. I hope a bit of it might rub off on me.

The big prizes are for Religious Knowledge, and Grady wins the top prize by the length of the straight. The Dr Frank Dunworth Memorial Prize donated by his parents is his for another year. There isn't a parable he can't parrot. Old Macdonald nearly has to prise him away from Old Cheese's ring, which his lips seem to engulf. All the goody-two-shoes who win prizes for Religious Knowledge get their prizes first. They're all hardcover books with pictures. The top-shelf books from Angus and Robertson. It takes forever to get down to Third Grade Gold. Then there are awards for the Prefect, and Our Lady's Society and Holy Name Society, all of which Grady wins in a canter, then the Cadet Club Honours for best marching and stuff. Then Old Macdonald announces Paul Aloysius Simpson as this year's winner of the Reverend Brother E.C. Fields Memorial Prize, donated by Mr and Mrs G. Bussel. Simmo has to walk the entire length of the Town Hall and up the stairs before genuflecting and kissing Old Cheese's ring for hours. We agreed earlier that it would be a hoot if he really prolonged the kissing, and everyone on stage gets really fidgety as Simmo is on his knees crouched over Gilroy's hand for about two or three minutes, until Old Cheese pulls it away. I have to clap my hand over my mouth to suppress the giggles. The whole auditorium is smiling. Everyone but Old Cheese, for the first time in his life.

But even better comes next. This is the one we're all waiting for, and a couple of seats in front of me The Bike and Grantie keep turning around and winking as Simmo finds his way back while licking his lips. The Mathematics Prize this year, announces Old Macdonald, is awarded to Roger Ng. Who? cries out

The Bike anonymously. Old Macdonald falls straight in. Roger Ng. Almost everyone immediately starts saying to themselves, Roger Ng, Roger Ng, Roger Ng, until it's almost audible, and suddenly the whole audience is cracking up and pulling themselves to severe attention. Rogering. We keep saying it over and over again. It's a lucky thing Roger Ng is a dark Chinese from Hong Kong, otherwise he would have blushed bright red.

Mum isn't anywhere to be seen. I sort of half expect her not to come. After the Rogering I get up and check the foyer and go right out onto George Street, looking up and down, and rush back in to catch the Leadership, Study and Sport Prize. Since I've been in Sydney I've rarely had a letter from home. When I first arrived I watched with my heart in my throat as a Brother handed out the mail at teatime. Some kids got mail nearly every day from their brothers, sisters, parents, aunties and uncles. After a while I got so self-conscious about the lack of mail I wrote to myself and posted it down at Charing Cross. I beamed when my name was called by Mein Furner and chuckled while reading, as if for the first time. Dad gave me a couple of letters he'd written but forgot to post when I returned on holidays. It was a great way to catch up on the news. But even that has dried up over the years. Mum's nerves have got worse year by year. On my return to Albury during school breaks I enter the front door of the flat not knowing if Mum is there or in some hospital. She's worked her way from Melbourne Mercy to the Mater Miseracordiae in Sydney, and finally to Kenmore Psychiatric Hospital, which is usually the last station of the cross. But Dad has written to say she's fine and catching the Daylight Express to see me, and he's sorry both of them couldn't make it.

The French Prize and Debating Prize are done and my turn is coming up. The Town Hall door is wide open to the street and there's no sign of Mum. Finally Old Macdonald announces the Dux of College and I stand up and walk to the stage and go to run up the stairs when I trip on an electric wire connecting the speaker system and fall flat on my face, pulling the mike out of Old Macdonald's hands and sending it flying across the stage like a rat on a rope. I collect myself before collecting my prize from a shattered Headmaster. Old Cheese gives me the finger, the one with the ring, and I smooch it a while but worry about all the diseased lips that have been there that night.

Just as I get Colin Simpson's *The Big Country* from Old Macdonald, I see someone at the back of the Town Hall. Not in the auditorium but up in the gallery, near the rails upstairs, where the empty seats of the dress circle look down upon the stage. My eyes can't see because the lights of the stage make everything else a blur, but above it all I see Mum almost overbalancing across the rail, wrapped in her foxhead stole and a black coat opening over a bright red frock, waving her white-gloved hands above her head. She's made it, but her swaying is not just the stilettos on the balcony carpet. The dining car on the Daylight Express has been open and serving all the way from Albury to Sydney. Seppelts Cream Sherry by the smell of her when I kiss her cheeks in the corridor on the first floor. Oh Charlie, we're so proud. All I feel is the shame. God, I wish I was Chinese so you can't see how ashamed I feel.

I keep my views on Mum's drinking to myself but they fester inside. After a while the feeling just stays inside all by itself. It doesn't matter what's going on, there's this deep dark misery flowing underneath. At times I wish her dead.

She wants to meet all my friends. I try to say they aren't here but it's useless. We descend the marble stairs, one at a troubled time, into the extremely well-lit foyer where all my friends wait, heads arched towards us. No one notices the flask of Brandivino in her open purse before I manage to shut it. She is staying at the People's Palace in Pitt Street.

Shifting her from the steps of the Town Hall is like trying to remove the moon with a teaspoon. Parents and pupils pour out of the front doors and onto the street, looking for taxis in the traffic. Mum insists on meeting Old Macdonald, who lingers like a groupie while the Cardinal's Cadillac circles the block. When Mum drinks it has a physical effect on me. She seems to blur like a woodpecker in flight near a tree. It's some kind of weird osmosis where my vision starts seeing double, as if the umbilical cord is a drinking straw. My speech slurs when I introduce her to the extent that people lean sideways as if to say, What was that? I'm taking my mother on board.

Old Macdonald guides Mum down the steps by the elbow. You don't get to be Headmaster if you don't have people skills. He's a people person to his fingertips. In the street Mum suggests a pot of tea, and the three of us—Simmo, Mum and me—hold hands, Mum in gloves, across George Street. Simmo and I order spiders with double ice creams. Mum has tea fortified with a flourish of the flask. We compare our prize books, which still have the prices written in pencil on the inside jackets. There's a scroll stuck over each title page with room left for the name of the prize, the subject and the winner. I've also picked up the Physics prize which is a thin volume of the poetry of Judith Wright. The English prize is the life of Madame Curie. There's little coordination between the Brothers who buy the books and the Brothers in charge of sticking in the handwritten scrolls.

Mum is nodding off at table so Simmo kindly picks up the bill and we escort Mum down the street and around the corner. She wants to do something, quickly. She scampers up a dark lane off Liverpool Street into the shadows. Simmo and I wait. Soon a trickle then a stream of liquid runs downhill out of the shadows along the gutter. A passing headlight reveals Mum on her haunches, poised over the kerb with all her underwear still in place. We pretend nothing has happened. We're soon inside the bright foyer of the People's Palace. Simmo and I tuck her in way after she falls asleep. The matter is never mentioned again. It's a bonus having such great mates as Simmo.

* * *

Moffitt rereads the Riot Act to us outside the Town Hall. We can make our own way back to college, but there'll be hell to pay if we get there later than midnight.

There's nothing emptier than city streets at night. Somehow the absence of things makes what's left all the more hollow. It's as if you can feel what's missing. An empty classroom is emptier than an empty closet.

Four boys in blue blazers and boaters, after dark in George Street with coins in their pockets and growling in their stomachs and mischief in their minds, is a sight to see. In seconds flat we are all sitting in the gutter in Park Street with four burgers with the works from the late night Greek café, juice running down our legs, laughing at Grantie who couldn't find his money in the café and went from pocket to pocket while the Greek held his burger in a brown paper bag. Grantie told him to hold his horses a minute. The Greek blew up. Vot you mean, horses? It is beef. Only the best beef. Grantie was stunned, and none of us got it for a minute, and then we all burst out laughing. We couldn't stop. The Greek shooed us all out into the street, swearing in Greek and telling us never to come back.

Charles Waterstreet

Life doesn't get much better than this. I am laughing so hard that a mouthful of whatever it is shot out over the road with a stream of lettuce and mayonnaise in its wake. The giant black and white posters of LBJ seem to break into a smile. An occasional taxicab slows down going by, and speeds off when it becomes apparent what we are. Every time one of us says Hold your horses we all dissolve in cackles until our eyes weep and our noses run.

Light rain has begun to fall, but not enough to wet the ground under parked cars, where patches of dry bitumen make the dark street look a bit like a chequer board from the angle where we sit. From around the Woolworth's corner a strange figure appears and disappears between the parked cars like a comic strip. A small hunched old man in a black greatcoat with a blood-red fez on his head, pushing a dirty pram with bicycle wheels. The collar of his coat flares up over what must be his neck, but his chin is tucked into his chest. He wears dirty fingerless black gloves that house jet black hands that even Solvol sandstone couldn't clean. His nails are edged like sympathy cards. The lighting of Woolies window makes him even more unreal. We stop giggling in our hands and simultaneously arise from the gutter and walk over to this mysterious figure moving slowly up Park Street.

Simmo is first as usual. Whatcha got in there? The black Turk doesn't stop or acknowledge us in any way. He keeps pushing his home-made pram. Between the bicycle wheels is a battered iron chest the size of an apple box. It's padlocked shut with a large brass Lockwood. He keeps moving slowly. We circle him like Indians around a wagon. Whatcha got in there? Come on, show us. Dead babies, I betcha. The handles flare up like a startled stallion. He stops when The Bike stands in his way but says and does nothing. Simmo flicks the lock with his fingers but it just clanks against the sides. I say he must have treasure in there which he's been saving for years. We've all seen him from time to time around the inner city, pushing his cart through traffic, through crowds. Going nowhere in particular. After a while he became part of the city's furniture, like bus stops and toilets. But the four of us know we have to find out what is in that box tonight or else.

It isn't that we planned to bump him over and push his pram into Hyde Park under the lights, where Simmo gets a branch from a strong tree and prises open the flap from the lid. It's something we just have to do. Something unstated has overcome us and we act in a conspiracy of our unbetter angels.

Jesus H. Christ, says Grantie as we stand in silence glaring into the iron box. The distressed Turk has regained his short legs and is crossing the street in a flurry. There is no treasure. No dead babies. Just another spoked wheel. Inside the iron box the Turk has pushed around the streets for year after year is just another wheel. Simmo calls him Our Lady of Perpetual Motion.

We all put our watches back ten minutes and wave our wily wrists under Mein Furner's nose saying Just in time, eh?

The lights are still on in the locker room but everybody else is in bed. We get into our pyjamas relatively quickly except for the occasional Hold your horses and round of giggles. I take my book to bed with the flashlight. Inside the front cover is a placard with blue embossed printing and my name in blue-black ink. One of the younger Brothers' steady hands. The book itself looks a bit of a bore, and before too long Simmo has passed me the folded page from *Pix* with Christine Keeler sitting backwards on a curved chair. With flashlight in one hand and Christine Keeler flat on the floor under the bed and myself in the other, I take my turn with her. When I'm done I fold her and pass her on to The Bike. The Brothers must wonder why we go through so many hankies when none of us has a cold.

By the time I fall asleep there is a faint scent of White King cleaner in the air of the dormitory. None of us will be up for Communion tomorrow. Confession for the boarders is on Thursdays, and most of us make Communion on Friday but by Monday a few of the older boys stay in their seats and don't join the queue for their bits of Jesus. By Wednesday none of the repeating boarders leave their pews. The Brothers must wonder what mortal sins boys could commit without them being wise to it. Funny thing is that not one Brother ever misses Communion. There are never any late night drive-in confessions, so how do they do it? How in the hell do they survive the night without even thinking about it? It must be a fine line between a wet dream and an act of impurity. It's one they constantly criss-cross. Of course they don't have the folded photo of Christine Keeler that Simmo keeps under his mattress.

Mum

Dr Twomey again schedules Mum for admission to Kenmore Hospital shortly after her return to Albury from the People's Palace. This is her second admission.

On admission she is covered in small bruises and on the verge of DTs. She vomits for twelve hours and is put on intravenous fluids. Dr Tooth prescribes Antabuse to be taken every morning. It is designed as a deterrent to alcohol use and is used in the management of chronic alcoholism. If taken with alcohol it causes an adverse reaction. The upper body, including the face, chest and limbs, flushes bright red. This is followed by sweating, palpitations, tachycardia, dyspnoea, hyperventilation and pounding headaches. The throat constricts and uncontrollable coughing begins. A fear of dying may follow. After the flushing the skin becomes pallid and the patient suffers nausea and cramping. This lasts up to four hours. Thankfully, it is not addictive. Dr Tooth believes that the anti-depressant Amitriptylline should be continued indefinitely.

Mum's condition is called 'nerves' by all the family. It covers a multitude of ills. Her case history records her conditions variously as acute psychotic state, delusionary, hallucinatory, religious mania, alcoholic, reactive depression, chronic depression, manic depression, neurotic, psychotic depression with secondary alcoholism. With such a cornucopia of conditions, nerves seem easier and perhaps more accurate. She is so addicted to pills that my brothers and sister fetch them from the chemist for her in heaped armfuls thrown into her bedside drawer. In the depths of a long depression the only solids she eats are Relax-a-Tabs, Vincent's, Bex and Veganin.

Her life this year is a tag game, back and forth, home to hospital and back home again. She begins to build up her physical health again.

Citizens
Welcoming
Committee

The news of President Johnson's visit to Australia is broken by some devilishly keen reporting by a journalist at the *Daily Mirror* whose byline states 'by Gerry Stone who telephoned the White House'. The cloud of secrecy has been penetrated by the unpredictable chance call of a bored pressman. It's now on for young and old.

The State Premier, Mr Robin Askin, sets up the Citizens Special Welcoming Committee which immediately announces that the slogan for the President's visit will be Make Sydney Gay for LBJ. The Committee is chaired by the Lord Mayor of Sydney, Alderman Armstrong, who strongly denies he has been snubbed when the Premier announces that the gala reception will be held at the New South Wales Art Gallery instead of the Town Hall. The Lower Town Hall has in fact, he claims, been booked for a concert in support of a Health Week exhibition. The Committee also comprises Mr Asher Joel, a Sydney public relations genius, and Mr Clarrie Garth, the City Council Superintendent of Parks and Gardens. The guiding hand of the Premier is seen by cynics to lie behind the choice of the Art Gallery. But they are soon muffled when the Mayor reveals that someone did ring up the Town Hall, did inquire about its availability without identifying themselves, and promptly hung up.

The Premier drops public transport fares for the day of the visit for all schoolchildren in New South Wales, provided two simple conditions are met. Firstly an adult, be it a parent, schoolteacher, clergyman, scoutmaster or anyone else of standing, has to take responsibility. Secondly, stationmasters have to be notified by 4 p.m. on the Wednesday before the parade. The Minister for Transport wants the efficient deployment of rolling stock. The Premier wants the accent to be on youth, and they are to be given pride of place at the front of the barricades lining the presidential motorcade route. Five hundred seats are made available for the physically disabled in Art Gallery Road, and 100 seats for old age pensioners on the northern pavement of Liverpool Street between College Street and Elizabeth Street. Organisers ask pensioners to bring their medical, pension or travel concession cards with them to dissuade conmen. A special location has been chosen for the blind, equipped with extra loudspeakers, out of the way so as not to waste valuable space but abundant with Braille banners and bunting. They are placed near bands so they can be entertained until the President drives past. Those both blind and deaf will have to look out for themselves.

The Committee makes hay while the sun shines. An instant bush setting is organised for the Art Gallery, with thousands of native blooms, potted palms, grass tufts and gum trees to provide an authentic landscape. To top it all off kangaroos, wallabies and koalas are going to be brought from Taronga Park Zoo to feed on the temporary foliage. Mr Joel announces that Sydney will have the best-organised spontaneous welcome the President will ever have in the whole wide world.

No effort to impress the President will be spared: 10,000 balloons bearing the words Welcome to President Johnson, 100,000 lapel badges for children with a picture of LBJ and crossed Australian and American flags, 5000 posters distributed to retailers, a veritable snowstorm of tickertape with Hooray for LBJ at key positions along the way, the issue of invitations to boy scouts and girl guides to be in uniform, and at the airport a thousand children wearing Texan-style cowboy hats. Mr Joel says he wants the President to feel he is in Texas—a real Australian welcome.

Almost every hour in the week before the visit a new

announcement is made. The Bike keeps the rest of the boarders informed of goings-on in the outside world by knocking off his parents' newspapers in the afternoons during pantry raids. We devour the television programmes although we can't watch at school but are informed the next day by boggle-eyed day boys. We know nearly every skit on The Mavis Bramston Show without ever seeing an episode.

The motorcade is to bypass the 'street of smells' from Mascot Airport—O'Riordan Street with its tanneries and sewage treatment works—and travel along Anzac Parade, which is to be renamed President Johnson's Way for the day. Sixteen bands will play at key points along the 14-mile route. All they need to do is to agree on a tune. Ten tons of tickertape are printed, enough to stretch from Sydney to Washington, and cut up into 8 by 1 inch strips; 150,000 flags on 6000 yards of specially treated linen will be printed, and, as a special treat for Lady Bird, a thousand pigeons will be released at Queens Square as a welcoming gesture. The Citizens Welcoming Committee convene and decide that the pigeons will not be fed on the three days before the Presidential procession so as not to blemish the salute to Lady Bird or rain on the President's parade. Organisers are worried that pigeons are no respecters of persons and that the famous bubble-top Lincoln convertible will be a target for the excited birds. A few days off food won't hurt them, says Soon-to-be-Sir Asher Joel. He isn't a member of the Legislative Council for nothing. It's the New South Wales Upper House—full of upper people elected only by those who own land in the state. Those without property can only vote for the aptly named Lower House. The Upper House is for the landed gentry who really have a stake in the state.

Marching girls and drum majorettes will give a display at Queens Square, which is to be decorated with a million flowers donated by the city's citizens. There is little Premier Henry Bolte of Victoria can do but decry the antics and stunts of the Askin Government.

The bubble-top has been rebuilt from the ground up. It has been armoured, re-armoured, made bullet proof and made double bullet proof. It has been installed with such a communication system that it is a rolling extension of the White House. When the President is inside there is not a rifle in the world powerful enough to penetrate the car's hide. The glass itself has been specially developed by the US Secret Service. Its thickness has never been disclosed but is estimated by reporters extending thumb and forefingers as one and a half inches. The car can cruise at speeds up to 80 mph because of special drag devices built into the suspension. Its boot has two transmitters in case one breaks down. The car is patched through a series of relay stations directly to the Pentagon, and is fitted with a signal-scrambling device which can make Johnson's prose sound like so much gibberish to anyone eavesdropping. It also carries the Hot Line to the

Kremlin and the nuclear trigger in case the commies decide to attack while the President is out of the country. A typical Soviet trick.

Sea vessels are stationed every 250 miles between the US West Coast and Australia in case Air Force One crashes. Frogmen will scour Sydney Harbour for mines and G-men with stethoscopes will check the Art Gallery for bugs. Armed guards will be hidden in rooftops along President Johnson's Way in constant two-way radio touch with the mastermind, Rufus W. Youngblood. Advance cars of armed agents will precede the President's car, which will contain at least one armed agent. Seven agents will be in the car behind, one facing the rear. Air Force One will have a fighter escort at all times. The cream of the state's CIB and other plain-clothes detectives will liaise with the G-men to provide cover for the President. The *Sun-Herald* reports that policemen on duty will be served with special snacks: three sandwiches and a can of soft drink to each man. The President's own medical practitioner, Dr Bushby, will be on hand with two large medical kits to administer on the spot treatment in any medical emergency, from heart attack to a bullet wound. A food taster is usually in attendance with the President. US agents are going to watch the preparation of all food in the kitchens in Australia. All waiters will be vetted by agents under the direct control of Youngblood. Only selected drinks will be served. The President's clean green pyjamas, with a handkerchief tucked in the pocket, will be kept constantly ready on the bed in the private cabin of Air Force One. Between touchdowns, Mr Johnson will change into pyjamas, sleep instantly and wake refreshed.

Posses of agents fan out over the entire Pacific in advance of his trip. Australia is no stranger to attempted political assassinations. We follow on America's coat-tails in nearly everything under the sun. The government rejected the Royal, the Goanna, the Galah, the Phar Lap and the Bunyip for the dollar as a currency. Earlier in the year a nineteen-year-old Sydney factory worker, Peter Kocan, plotted to make himself as famous as his idol Lee Harvey Oswald. He wrapped a shortened .22 rifle in brown paper and headed off to an anti-con-scription rally addressed by opposition leader Mr Arthur Calwell. He fired at point-blank range outside Mosman Town Hall, and contrary to popular belief that Australians are natural born jungle fighters, he completely missed and hit the car window, which shat-tered all over Mr Calwell. Kocan went to a mental institution and wound up as Australia's most success-ful poet.

Mr Calwell himself, as my Aunt Faith often says, is no oil painting, but he demands equal time with the Prime Minister to put his anti-Vietnam position to the President. Mr Calwell had left his mark on history when as Immigration Minister during the 1940s he said that two Wongs do not make a white. He also told Parliament that no red-blooded Australian wants to see a chocolate-coloured Australian. There is something uniquely Australian about him, as if a white cockatoo had been tarred and unfeathered, left in a dust storm and then someone had plonked an old pair of grandpa's spectacles on it. When the Speaker of Parliament resigned Mr Calwell advised him to accept the psychiatrist's advice to the kleptomaniac: Take things quietly. He is the antithesis of his deputy, the tall handsome urbane Mr Gough Whitlam. He won't last long. He'll never be described as windswept and interesting, more flyblown and buggered.

The Sevenths

The last footy games of the season have been pushed forward to the Friday before LBJ's visit. We are to face the traditional enemy to boot. St Joseph's College is chock-a-block with hairy-legged farm boys with bull necks and timber-cutting arms, all the way down to the Sevenths. I play football as well as the next boy, as long as he is also in the Sevenths. But Joeys guys live and breathe football. Simmo reckons they go to bed in scrum formation. Football is their religion. And the thing they hate worse than losing is Waverley College. Even in the Sevenths, Joeys play like it's a jihad between Catholics. And they aren't afraid to lay in a bit of the slipper. If you find yourself at the bottom of a collapsing scrum you expect to get out covered in sprig marks from arsehole to breakfast time. They aren't anything like love bites. Civil wars are always more vicious than foreign wars for the same reason. Joeys never tackle Scots or Cranbrook guys like they do

Waverley guys. When Catholics turn on each other like that it's little wonder that Protestants run the country.

Brother Moffitt has the Sevenths trained to the minute but not a second longer. We're out of puff by then. Except for The Bike, we do team push-ups from the knees. It's hard enough walking around with my weight on two legs let alone lifting it with only my arms. If we look fierce in the Sevenths school photo it's because we'd all placed our hands behind the back of our arms and pushed them out until the camera flashed and we let our stomachs down and breathed out in a huge gulp for air. The Bike could easily have made the Fifths or even Thirds, but he runs dead in games just to be with the rest of us. That's real team spirit—something that Moffitt bellows we'll need in spades against Joeys. Most of us are exhausted halfway through the warm-up.

The Joeys team look like Old Boys. I say we should check their birth certificates. But those farm boys from the back of Bourke age quickly in the desert sun. They look like they'd pulled the plough through the dried mud flats before they could walk. Moffitt has us doing star jumps, where we're supposed to clap our hands above our heads and jump and then spread our arms and legs out like the points of stars. It's quite apparent that this exercise does not put the fear of God into the Joeys' Sevenths when they laugh as we jump and clap and fall over. But this is 1966 and we don't want to be sports stars doing star jumps. We want to be pop stars doing groupies. There are no groupies at the Sevenths games at Queens Park.

Moffitt delights in physically humiliating us. He does one-arm push-ups. Simmo bets him a leave pass for a weekend that he can walk from one side of the oval to the other on his hands. Moffitt laughs and shakes hands on it. Simmo shakes his shoulders limbering up and trembles his arms down to his hands. He then bends over and puts his hands under his boots and walks like that over to the other side of the oval. We holler and hoot and Moffitt says it didn't count. But we know it did.

This is to be our last game of the year and probably our life. It would be good to go out on a win. But it's nine o'clock in the morning and most of our team still have crusts of sleep in their eyes and yawn through Moffitt's pep talk. Many of us are sapped of energy through having a wet dream last night. I'd spent months dreading coming to Waverley College for fear of wetting the bed and now as I'm leaving I'm wetting it all over again, but in a different way. It's such a waste, the wet dream, because most times you can't remember them and the only evidence is that your willie is Velcroed to the bed sheet and it hurts like hell when you pull it away, like a Bandaid strip.

Although it's late October the chunky grass of No 2 oval Queens Park is dewy wet and cold. Bursts of fog come out of our mouths and into the tunnels of fingers we make in an effort to keep warm. Playing second row on a Friday is not a great idea. Breakfast is either baked beans in tomato sauce or baked beans without tomato sauce. Putting my head down between Bodel and Edgar's hips may keep my ears warm but offers no protection to my nose when someone farts. With Simmo packed in behind me there is no room to move when the baked beans go off. Hell is having chilblains in your ears and your head between Bodel and Edgar's hip bones at 9.30 in the morning in October, with pudgy Joeys boys' fingers coming at your face trying to gouge your eyes out and the scrum moving about, each movement meaning that the top part of your ear goes one way and the lobe the other. I'm turning into a vegetable, one cauliflower ear at a time.

Moffitt shouting Push, push! and my arm around Hinchcliffe on second row, and the smell of Dencorub, sweat, moist farts, dirty underwear, boot polish, cheap soap sitting in your nose while you hold your breath—which makes it really difficult to push push back harder and harder, and the Waverley scrum starts going backwards. With a tremendous burst of energy we push back at Moffitt's Push, push! and out of the forest of legs in the middle of the front row of Joeys I see the second rower holding what appears to be a salt and pepper shaker. What sort of weird thinking is that? Better for tasting Waverley boys' heads! His hand crosses the scrum line into our second row and he starts shaking it. Instinctively I open my eyes wider and take a big lungful of air. Almost as one the Waverley pack rises in a huge slow-motion fit of sneezing. Moffitt thinks we're laughing and starts calling for control, and everyone has their hands on their face while Joeys run up the other end of the field for another try.

If anyone in the Firsts gets a crook knee or pulled muscle during the game Old Macdonald gets a few boarders to donate their rosaries with Lourdes water contained at the intersection of the beads. There is a raindrop of Lourdes water in a small glass and lead capsule in each rosary. Old Macdonald breaks through the glass gently with a penknife he carries at the bottom of the long side pocket of his habit and rubs it into the injured part. The miracle needs more Lourdes water if the first lot doesn't work. To be effective, Lourdes water works best by the teaspoon. Anything less is a waste of it. It takes about six sets of rosary beads to perform the miracle but I've seen it turn pulled hamstrings into place, untrick the trickiest knee, and it's a wonder with corked thighs. It is especially good with the unconscious, bringing them right round like the water from water bottles in Westerns. The Bike reckons that they couldn't have used Lourdes water in the West because it hadn't been invented yet. Our Lady of the Mount didn't appear at Lourdes until this century and by then all the West had been won from the Indians. But what are they doing in the movies? I ask. The Bike has a way of putting the quandary of life's conundrums just so. They're just actors, he says.

Anyway the whole Waverley scrum look like they are bawling their eyes out when Georgina and her friend Katie appear under the goalposts when the Joeys half-back is digging a hole in the ground for the goal kick. I'm mightily pleased to see her but I think the sight of me pressing down one nostril and exhaling the contents of the other onto the grass with the comet tail of it falling onto my sleeves doesn't meet with her instant approval. We must be a sight of sore eyes, wandering about wiping our eyes and the boys from the backline trying to blow the bits of entrenched black pepper from crying sockets.

All of Georgina's earlier boyfriends played at 2.30 in the afternoon, in the Firsts, with hundreds of school kids, teachers, parents, friends and girlfriends up and down the sidelines cheering them on. She's the first of her kind to date someone not in the Firsts. Usually, if a girl strays it's to another position within the Firsts, like from half-back to inside centre. Many have nicknames based on the position of their boyfriends, and if someone gets dragged up from the Seconds the lucky newly promoted boy nearly always gets the chick. It's a sort of reward. Unofficial trophy girlfriends. Georgina has dropped like a brick to the Sevenths. Katie is the one who really sticks by her.

I fear she'll miss the shouts of the crowd on Saturday afternoons, in the middle of the game when everyone is called upon at some crucial time to give the school war-cry to lift the team's spirit out of the bottom of the trench. There's nothing like a hundred or so voices screaming the school war-cry at full pitch to make a guy dig deep into himself and go that extra yard, especially if Old Macdonald has rubbed him all over with Lourdes water or the relic of old saints if there were no beads with water. The school war-cry is not complex. Far from it. It's the school name spelt twice. When Moffitt or Old Macdonald calls for Double Waverley! it's a tremendous thing for the boys on the field to hear WW, AA, VV, EE, RR, LL, YY. The school's supporters are not great spellers, being from the school itself, or Old Boys or people like that. It really doesn't matter, because a Double Waverley even without the second e gets the boys on the field to perform small miracles.

Simmo screams out to Georgina and Katie for a Double Waverley while we are drying our eyes. Georgina looks gorgeous. I can't believe my luck. I'm totally in like with her. She's wearing black boots and a new green tartan mini-dress with a huge safety pin down the side. A black duffel coat with the hood up keeps the cold out. She looks like a wild Scottish monkess. Georgina and Katie start out slowly with a few Double Waverleys and keep them going while the whole Joeys team and our team get down on our hands and knees in a straight line across the field to look for The Bike's left-side contact lens. It must have fallen out with the crying from the pepper.

Moffitt loves organising this part of drill. On the far goal-line he lines his teams up, everyone on hands and knees with straight backs in a perfect line enforced by Moffitt's boot if encroaching hands go over the goal-line. At the count of three, the line moves forward on one hand and knees with the other hand's index finger going into the mouth to wet the tip of it and then tap it lightly in the moist grass immediately in front of you for The Bike's left contact lens. When we've wet and licked and tapped the area immediately in front, the line moves forward slightly, like a search party of regimental seagulls combing the beach for worms. By the time we reach Georgina's goal-line at the other end without one wet finger finding anything but cigarette butts and bottle tops, we look like we've all played a game anyway. Our knees are grassy knolls, our index fingers are wet and frozen, and the girls hoarse from scores of mis-spelt Double Waverleys. We had 'em on their knees for most of the game, crows Simmo in triumph. Playing in the Sevenths is not my idea of living on the edge. The only way it can be described as a contact sport is when The Bike lost his.

The Sevenths have a proud history this season: no team has ever scored in the three figures against us, and Simmo scored a try against the St Aloysius school early in the season. I reckon that didn't count for much because it's hard for Aloysius boys to tackle while their hands are clasped in prayer.

After brushing the grass off my knees I walk up to Georgina as ruggedly as I can. She puckers up but everyone's perving so I go down on one knee and say

Your Grace a la Old Cheese and kiss her hand. She refuses to let my hand go and I have to practically engage in a tug of war to get it off her. I don't mind holding hands, as long as no one's watching.

It's about half a mile uphill from Queens Park back up Salisbury Road to the school. There isn't a sweeter sound in the world than the click click click of sprigged footy boots on the concrete footpath as we make our way back. Georgina and Katie come as far as Theo's Hot Chips and Sandwiches at Charing Cross, where we hush-order secret hamburgers—it's a Friday and Moffitt'd have a fit if he knew we were at Theo's in the first place, with girls in the second place, and with meat in our mouths on a fish-only Friday. But meat never tastes better than on a Friday, especially in Lent, when every day is supposed to be a fast day. I gave up fasting for my last Lent.

Theo's Hot Chips and Sandwiches is full to bursting with Waverley boys gobbling down meat as if their lives depended on it. Slices of camp pie, devon, ham, German sausage and even fists of peperoni, for Theo's handmade pizzas go down the gullet in fits of rampant and mass mortal sinning. We all make ourselves at home in a corner booth after Simmo pisses off some junior boys one at a time by their ears.

I am beginning to learn the ways of the world of women very quickly. While teenage boys tend to hunt in packs, girls tend to hang in pairs. Girls like Georgina, beautiful and sought-after by nearly everyone, usually have a best friend like Katie, fat and if not plain or even ugly then just plain ugly—as if one is the painting and the other the frame. I don't know if the better-looking one makes a point of befriending the other to make herself look better or whether it's the other way round and the plain one hopes to eat the crumbs off her queen's table. And the other thing I notice is that, try as Georgina might, no one is ever keen to join us on a double date with Katie. So if we get any time together it's like Sell-Out Sunday at Batrouney's Auction Yard: buy one, get one free. Take out Georgina and get to spend time with Katie for free.

It isn't so bad because if the truth be known, and I'm damn sure it won't, I'm a little bit afraid to be truly alone with Georgina because I might have to step up to the plate some day, and despite all the reading and talking in the world, I still fear going all the way, whatever that really means. It's one thing with my fingers walking on tiptoe down her back and up again, with her quick correcting hand, but it's another altogether to actually be allowed, invited even, into that black bushy Garden of Eden not with just my inky fingers but cockfirst and balls following. It's nigh even too much to contemplate. I am sure that the best part is thinking about it and bragging, but not really doing it. Maybe I can't, and all in all it would be best not to know that.

We chat about the big day out tomorrow, when the President will be coming to Sydney all the way from

Canberra in Air Force One. Georgina is as effervescent as one of Theo's fresh spiders just after he's plonked a scoop of vanilla ice cream into a tall glass of Coke. She bubbles and froths and runs over the sides. The same thing is going on inside my tummy.

Another thing I've learned about chicks is this. Less is more. More or less. What I mean is that the less flesh you actually see, the more you want. A one-piece Speedo swimsuit on a girl just after she's finished doing laps at the Bondi surf-pool looks better than even the tiniest of tiny bikinis at the south end of Bondi. With Georgina, the thing that gives me the horn more than anything is that small strip of skin between the top of her black boots just below the knee and the bottom of her tartan dress. She has well-worn knees for a Greek. I fear she's spent some time on her knees with the boys of the backline of the Firsts.

Sitting in Theo's, in the last booth before the kitchen, you can see her knees under the bench if you lean right back and look down your nose. You can see the mottled blue flesh above the knees pressed down on the seat and pushing out like a punched-in pillow. How I long to place my hand on one—and then I do. Grantie is reading a joke from his well-worn and faded list, and after I throw my hands up in glee one falls on Georgina's knee and clamps shut, not moving. She turns her helmeted head to the side and bats her big blue mascaraed false eyelashes at me, and I think I'm in heaven. She doesn't move my hand. I leave it there for

what seems like hours. It sweats like a pig, and moisture forms in puddles in the space between my hand
and her knee and drips down her leg into her boot.

Simmo orders a super-large serving of Theo's chips,
which he lays flat out on the Formica table in the
middle of the booth. It's so piping hot the ink words
on the newspaper wrapping scream out Ouch and Ooh.
The Bike performs open heart surgery by unplucking
the Scotch tape and tumbling open the chips by pulling
the newspaper in careful small jerks until the sizzling
chips lie heaped upon each other like fish at the bottom
of a dragnet. Squirts of water-thinned tomato sauce
from plastic containers cool them down in long criss-
crossed spatters. My right hand only leaves Georgina's
knee to pick up the burnt end of a single chip to dab
it into the pool of sauce and get Georgina to blow air
on it before lobbing it down, burning my throat. My
greasy and sweaty palm returns to the chubby ledge of
skin. Her knee is now as grimy as the bottom pane of
glass on the back door at Preston's Prestige Motor
Works and Body Shop.

Even Theo's Hot Chips and Sandwiches is going gay
for LBJ. Through the mirage above the chips, like heat
haze above hot country roads, you can see ghosty
posters of President Johnson and Harold Holt smiling
at each other over crossed national flags. We all think
Theo's ten-gallon white hat is a bit too much, especially for a Greek fish and chip seller. Even Mrs Theo
and Little Theo have the big hats on. Mind you, none

of us boys have any political views about the visit, but we all know LBJ is no JFK. But Georgina has plans to join the anti-Vietnam demonstrators tomorrow. She has eyes for Bobby Kennedy, even though he never played in Waverley's First Fifteen and has about a hundred children. If Katie wears the T-shirt she has in her hand-bag proclaiming Make Love Not War, Simmo says, she'll be charged with false advertising.

Suddenly Georgina gets all serious and removes my hand and says that it's a crime that the Yanks are in Vietnam, and that LBJ is the biggest criminal of all. She sure is ballsy for a 5 foot 4 inch girl in leather boots. As I'm still at school, even though repeating, there's no chance I want to go fighting in the jungles of Vietnam, but I'm happy enough to cheer on those who do. I'm prepared to go all the way with LBJ as long as I don't have to go myself. As far as Georgina's protest is concerned, I'll go any way she wants as long as I can put my hand back on her knee.

President Johnson took Canberra by storm yester-day. He handed out scores of ballpoint pens at Fairbairn Airport to waiting crowds. The President had sneaked into the Canberra Rex Hotel by the back entrance, leaving hundreds of protesters outside holding placards with what the chip-grease-stained newspaper says were generally anti-American themes. Barbecue LBJ. Burn War Plans Not Asians. Some truly Australian demon-strators held signs with I Like Beer or God Save Ireland. The only sad note of the President's first day in

Canberra occurred when a pedestrian was killed by a scaffolding truck driving to put up giant photos of LBJ.

Georgina is giving everyone a piece of her mind, which prompts Simmo to say she'd better be careful because there won't be much left. That sort of comment really gets her going and I sense that eating meat on Friday is about as close to a mortal sin as I'm going to get today.

We clink our way back up Salisbury Road to school while the girls plan their big demo for tomorrow.

Going Gay
for LBJ

Brother Mein Furner's thunderclapping hands start at the doorway from the locker room and roll relentlessly up and down the aisles of beds in the dormitory until bursting right next to my left ear. Boys in crumpled pyjamas fall out of their beds like rain to their knees. We wait for our morning glories to go down a little and out of the reach of Mein Furner's downcast eyes. Our lips move but not in prayer. We're more likely to be thinking of Little Pattie than Our Pater. We're more likely to be softly singing Last Train to Clarksville or Spicks and Specks or Sunshine Superman or Eleanor Rigby than Hail Mary. The Bike has a little red transistor that the beds immediately in the vicinity of his can hear in the pitch dark of night above the gentle moaning of boys and their heartfelt hands.

I am stiff and sore from the big game against St Joseph's. My knees jump for their lives on reaching the floor in mock prayer. I steal a leaf from Simmo's book and pull my pillow off the bed and throw it under my knees. The tip of my index finger aches. Football injuries come in all shapes and sizes in the Sevenths.

Mein Furner is shaking the last of the sleepyheads by the shoulders before pulling the blankets and sheets off the beds as quickly as a magician. Curled-up boys slide like snakes out of beds in grumpy silence.

* * *

Meanwhile, every employee at Mascot International Airport has brought their vacuum cleaner from home to work. From dawn they pace up and down the tarmac with long electrical leads in a last-minute effort to ensure that there will be no dust where the presidential party will alight.

Clouds dare not show their faces on this Day of Days lest they too are sucked into the eager mouths of the army of deadly Hoovers and Electroluxes patrolling the airport.

* * *

Some boys keep rosary beads in the top pocket of their pyjama tops wrapped inside a snotty handkerchief. They fumble with the beads on their knees, not to pray but to appear to pray. It is hard for Brother Mein Furner to question their fervour when they have rosary beads in their hands. Appearances count for everything in school life. Real life takes place between our ears and between our legs. It's hard sometimes not to feel that while we pray, the Furner preys on us.

Soon forty boys from our dorm line up in single file for showers. We want to look our best for President Johnson. Some of the country boys shave before the long mirror, leaving black-speckled foam in the hand-basins. They use razor blades. A few of us foam up like Father Christmas and run the Gillette over our cheeks and chins without the need of a razor blade. It's more for practice for when the time comes. There are no black specks in the foam in the handbasin when I leave. A couple of the Greek boys will need to shave again before Air Force One touches down at 11 a.m.

Although it's Saturday, we put on our dark blue school uniforms. The sports stars wear their bright blue blazers with yellow badge and printed achievements on the right-hand side. There is no Sevenths blazer.

The locker room divides into two schools. The Brylcreem brigade wear their hair all shiny and sleek with teeth comb marks from ear to ear. I am in the moptop school of hair inspired by the Beatles and the Dave Clark Five, when the only time the hand goes near the head is to brush the hair from our eyes. It's more my style: do nothing. My hair has a mind of its own and grows in all directions. I leave it as well enough alone as Mein Furner allows.

You wouldn't believe that this brave band of boys is soon to be lured into town to wave flags before the most powerful man on earth and his missus. We'd have been more excited if it had been President Kennedy. Still, it's better than the Pope. At least there won't be a three-hour papal Mass and Communion en masse. Father Keneally often lapses back into Latin during morning Mass. It's hard to master the brand new Eighth Vatican II version without subtitles. Anyway, the old Latin somehow sounds holier with its singsong Et cum spirit tuo-tuo-oh. How we all yearn for those final words at the end of morning Mass: Go, the Mass has ended. Thank fucking Christ, we whisper to each other.

Amazingly, we nearly all go to Communion. I was too tired from the game and looking for The Bike's left lens to even think about unloading last night. Putting my hand on Georgina's knee was certainly not a mortal sin, even if I may have crossed the line in thought and maybe word. I give myself the benefit of the doubt on that one. I don't want to be left like a shag on a rock in the pew while everyone else takes Communion. We should greet the President in a state of grace.

The new chapel, made possible when plate after plate was passed around from Old Boy to Old Boy and not returned until it was overflowing with pound notes and pledges, has been built with the popular new white bricks. White brick housing developments are spreading like a rash over the green pastures outside Parramatta and all the way to Penrith at the feet of the Blue Mountains. The new chapel looks like an English cousin just arrived from the old country next to the granite and red brick old dormitory wing. There is something unreal about a chapel being bright and shiny with stained glass storeys high allowing all the sunlight inside. We hope God is colour-blind because the Brothers certainly are. Churches are supposed to be old, dark and deeply mysterious places where you can barely see so you can nod off at any tick of the clock.

The altar is made out of stainless steel, if you don't mind. I yearn for thick sirloin marble slabs. I miss Albury's St Pat's and its cedar pulpit, belltower and pews. All this light makes snoozing almost impossible. It's so bright the pimples on the back of Grantie's neck, hidden in the hair just above his collar, glow red and yellow. They look as big as boils when he turns his head. If Nana were here she'd have a couple of Vegemite jars heating up in hot water to bung onto his neck to draw them out. Probably draw some nearby organs and bone marrow too. She sucked out my boils when I was young with the enthusiasm of a missionary among a newly discovered tribe in New Guinea. I've got craters up and down my body where boils came out and into hot Vegemite jars looking like giant teeth with black and yellow roots. Jars are good but the recent invention of Magnaplasm put a lot of grandmas out of work.

Women love getting stuff out of your body. Georgina can be pashing me one minute and the next she's at the crevice of my nose with her index fingers pushing the bejesus through my pores. Aunt Faith loves nothing better than checking my back for blackheads and pinching the heads off them with tweezers. It must be some kind of mating ritual, but that would count out Nana and Aunt Faith. It's a female thing. I hate it. If you get right up close to a mirror and push your fingers between the gap at the side of your nose, yellow squirts of pus come out like tiny bits of toothpaste.

The old boy who designed the new chapel at the usual discount cut a few corners when building the roof. The corrugated tin amplifies the pitter-patter of light rain through the chapel until it sounds like the charge of the Light Brigade down Dean Street on the tar. A storm makes it sound as if we're under attack. The Brothers sit at the back of the chapel so as to watch over us and to nod off quietly, unnoticed. But everyone looks to the high roof when the first spits of rain land, and pray that Sydney will not go grey for LBJ.

The clouds soon blow away after God has given the city a gentle hosing down. Sunlight lights up the great yellow pane of glass on the school side of the chapel. We all look as if we have jaundice for a while. Simmo pretends we've all suddenly turned Japanese, holding his fingers in the side sockets of his eyes and pulling them apart. The whole row is doing it before a cough from behind indicates Mein Furner is on the prowl.

Over a healthy breakfast of beans and rigid toast that breaks like super-sensitive crackers, we plan the day's escapades. Speaking of tangents, the word 'motorcade' conjures up the most phenomenal visions of black leather cops on bikes, fluttering flags on limousines, and shots ringing out from nowhere. Motorcade is a real twentieth-century word. It would have been impossible to have had a motorcade in the nineteenth century no matter how big the event. Horsecade just doesn't roll over the tongue quite right. Maybe carriagecade. Motorcade is *now*. Like transistors.

Dad recently sent me the *Border Morning Mail*; he was too busy to write so he cut out the middleman and just sent the local paper. A boatcade of twenty boats is to take part in the Hume Weir Aquatic Festival through Albury and Wodonga. It will really be a motorcade as the boats will be on the backs of trucks, but Albury is at the cutting edge of inland pleasure craft displays. Once Dad sent me a beer coaster in an envelope just to let me know he was thinking of me. Nothing written on it. Just the Fosters coaster. Brand new, though.

Simmo wonders aloud if Johnson will make a speech at the Art Gallery to match Kennedy's in Berlin. Ich bin ein Sydneysider. We all give various versions. The Bike says that one thing is clear: this visit marks the official declaration that we are the fifty-third state of

America. Fifty-first, I correct. It's true that the Queen is diminishing in indirect proportion as the Beatles rise. But Prince Charles is part Australian, isn't he? says Grantie. Just because he spent a term at fucking Timbertop doesn't make him one of us, I say.

The Queen never gets this much attention in Australia when she visits. Australia is growing up and leaving the shadow of Great Britain for the shadow of the United States. It isn't that we are being unfaithful. We just want to see other people. The Ealing Studios are no match for Hollywood. Prince Philip seems to have no life in him. President Johnson is larger than life. Certainly larger than life down under. The difference in the two is the stance. Prince Philip probably goes to bed with his hands clasped behind his back on his bum. Simmo says it's a variation of the Greek position. LBJ holds his hands over his head, outstretched, threatening to bear-hug you or lay you out, a Stetson in one hand, a pistol in the other. We all want to be in America without a doubt. England let us down in Singapore, in Europe, in the last Ashes tour. If it weren't for Princess Alexandra we'd secede. The English are our parents. The Americans are our mates. The English are exclusive, the Americans inclusive. Who wants to sleep at home when you can sleep over? We owe a lot to Great Britain but I can't think of anything right now.

Queen Elizabeth II has sent a telegram to the Prime Minister, conveying her regards for the Presidential visit.

Typical, I say; not even a phone call. It was probably sent by one of her minions. She doesn't even sign them.

We are going to town to see our first motorcade. A Presidential motorcade. Put that in your pipe and smoke it.

The President has taken Canberra in a storm if not by storm. In a terrifically emotional moment that seemed to bystanders to last hours, the President stood in front of a slouch-hatted soldier guarding the Cenotaph at the Imperial War Memorial. The soldier's rifle point was touching the ground, his hands folded on the butt, his head downcast. President Johnson poked out his hand to be shaken. The soldier did not flinch. The President held his empty hand there for an eternity before finally wiping a tear from his eye. Well done soldier! I am mighty proud of you. LBJ then moved on to the other three soldiers forming a square in resting on arms in reverse position. He offered each soldier an LBJ ballpoint pen. Although they politely declined, he placed one in each soldier's top pocket.

Not to be outdone by her husband, Lady Bird was driving back from a tree-planting ceremony when her limousine knocked over a mother and baby. Luckily it was Lady Bird's day, and both were relatively unhurt. Motorcades can be dangerous affairs.

It's time to come to Sydney. A crowd of well-wishers at Canberra Airport sing For He's A Jolly Good Fellow as Air Force One jets along the tarmac on its way to Sydney. Inside the 707 the President studies a map of Australia. It's labelled Victoria 1/3rd Texas; New South Wales slightly larger than Texas; Queensland 2× Texas; Northern Territory twice Texas; Western Australia 3× Texas; Tasmania 1/10th Texas; and ACT 13 times Washington DC. This visit puts Australia well and truly on the map.

* * *

Georgina and Katie are protesting the war at the Art Gallery, where the State Civic Reception is going to be held. Old Macdonald wants us to stand on the steps of St Mary's Cathedral even though the motorcade is not going past. What a fuckwit! Once we get out of the buses and into the crowd we're going to flee like bandits.

Brother Moffitt is in charge of transportation. He has us in the bus, with boaters and flags, by ten sharp. He too has in mind to countermand Old Macdonald's orders. There's no use going to St Mary's where the only glimpse of the President will be of his image on bunting or placards. He instructs the bus driver to take us to the Art Gallery if he can get through the traffic. Moffitt hangs off a passenger strap at the front and leads us in hymn. There's always time for a quick prayer or hymn, he says. That way you'll never fall behind. I reckon I'm way ahead for life.

Although clouds hung over Canberra like cartoon

balloons, the Sydney skyline is all blue screen. The Prime Minister's men have stuck a flying kangaroo on the side of Air Force One. On sighting it, LBJ tells Mr Holt that what he'd really like to do is go on a kangaroo shoot. He loves nothing better than to don a khaki shirt and pants, a Texan hat and western boots, and go hunting deer in the backwoods. He recently felled a buck with a single shot. Presidents of America have a long and proud history of sportsmanship. Kennedy was a yachtsman and pantsman. Eisenhower played golf. Johnson yearns to shoot a few roo before Vietnam peace talks in Manila.

Hail Queen of Heaven, the Ocean Star keeps the bus bouncing along Oxford Street until it comes to the part where it's been renamed President Johnson's Way. Thousands of people choke the footpaths along the way to the city. Brother Moffitt points the bus driver down Darlinghurst Road and through Kings Cross. Boys, boys, put your hands over your eyes! We peek through our fingers like Carmelite nuns through curtains.

Moffitt announces it's time for a prayer. Hail Mary full of grace, Pray that I put it in the right place. After Father Keneally told us to say a prayer for purity before taking a girl out on a date, Simmo made up this prayer for exactly such an occasion. Can you imagine actually saying a prayer before a date unless it's to ask God that she not get pregnant? These men of God have no idea when it comes to chicks. It's little wonder none of them is married.

Crowds gather along all Sydney's streets as if the motorcade were going to zigzag through town. Teams of police make sure they get the best positions to see. Some people slept overnight in sleeping bags along the route to ensure the best views. They awoke to find even craftier early birds have taken the kerbside for themselves. Milk crates are selling at a premium. Hawkers sell Turf Filter periscopes made of cardboard and mirrors for latecomers, kids and dwarfs. Schoolchildren are allowed to stand in front along the streets. Many took their old school uniforms out of the closet, brushed them down and set out for the city.

Soon-to-be-Sir Asher Joel and his support team have planned the parade route for the maximum exposure with the minimum risk. There was a scare overnight when a 28-year-old Croat who escaped from a mental hospital last Tuesday was spotted by an eagle-eyed detective using an Identikit picture. He had been diagnosed as a dangerous schizophrenic who had threatened high-level public servants in Sydney eleven months ago. LBJ would have been a great feather in one of his caps. Round-the-clock operations continued until midnight and restarted at six, when he was safely recaptured.

The Welcoming Committee is leaving no stone unturned. There had been a mini-disaster in New Zealand when the US Embassy staff and visiting reporters hired nearly all of Wellington's taxis, leaving most people without transport when Queen Elizabeth visited. Most of the Maori dancers at the airport had to hitch a ride in. Soon-to-be-Sir has all the rolling stock the railway has on the rails transporting visitors.

The Welcoming Committee has announced that a great Australian type of welcome will take place at the airport. Two 60-foot cranes will hold a 50-foot-long banner carrying the sign Welcome to Sydney—First City of Australia. Melbourne and Brisbane have similar banners. Sydney, said Soon-to-be-Sir, will go gay promptly at 11 a.m. On the route to Sydney, eight hundred members of the Returned Servicemen's League Youth Clubs have bands lined both sides of the road, playing different tunes. The President would notice that it sounded as if he were twisting the tuning knob on the limousine radio.

Cheer squads gather at Taylor Square under a sign saying Sydney's Gay for LBJ. They were chosen from the British Empire Boys Brigade and the New South Wales Fire Brigade. The colourful Police Boys Band play The Yellow Rose of Texas over and over and over. And over at the Elizabeth and Liverpool streets junction the entire New South Wales Pipe Band Association assembles under Sydney's Gay for You, LBJ. At the Town Hall steps, boy scouts and members of the Air League together with schoolchildren from as far as Bourke mass. In King Street a gigantic sign says The Eyes of Sydney Are Upon You. At Queens Square, the one-hundred-and-fifty-yard floral tribute of a million flowers reads Happy Stay Lady Bird in yellow daisies.

The thousand racing pigeons are caged, ready to be released as Lady Bird passes.

At the Domain around the Art Gallery the instant bush setting has been erected almost overnight, populated by Taronga Park Zoo's kangaroos, wallabies and koalas. Hopefully, LBJ has left his rifle at home.

After the reception there is to be a short motorcade down to Circular Quay, where the luxury VIP cruiser *Captain Phillip* will gently whisk the President, the Premier and the Ambassador and their current wives on a tour of beauty spots around the Harbour for lunch. Sydney Cove is banned to other pleasure craft and a four knot speed limit has been declared for the entire Harbour. Afterwards, the motorcade will retrace its way to Mascot and thence back to Canberra at 3 p.m. There can be no extra time lest Melbournians whinge about it.

Hundreds of speedboats are moored in choppy waters off Farm Cove. Thousands of women in bikinis cover their bodies in Johnson's baby oil for early summer tans. They are not allowed within four miles of the *Captain Phillip*, but many query whether the vice versa rule applies. Not with the missus aboard is the most common reply.

* * *

Miraculously, Moffitt has us within sight of the Art Gallery, on the fringes of the instant bush. He pushes the New South Wales Beagle Society members out of the way so we can line the roadway. Fifty-seven beagle dogs from all over the state have gathered with their owners in tribute to the President. Simmo and I look at them and then at each other and burst out laughing. We'd thought exactly the same thing. The beagles bear a canine but uncanny resemblance to President Johnson. It's as if fifty-seven of his illegitimate bastard dog children have come to see their father. It's terrific. We imagine them barking for their daddy when LBJ passes.

I ask everyone to keep their eyes peeled for Georgina. It's hard to see past your own nose in this crowd, pushing against the wire mesh surrounding the instant bush and its natural inhabitants. A swarm of G-men with shovels dig up around the instant trees and plants, looking for last-minute bombs. The foliage is potted in gallon tin cans of Swan Lager, which you can see clearly sticking out of the ground.

At Mascot the motorcade has been narrowed to nineteen vehicles. None of them was built locally. The pride of the fleet is the bubble-top Lincoln Continental. Rebuilt from the ground up in 1964 with double bullet-proofing, it is so heavy with armour it can travel at only 50 miles an hour tops, enough to make the twin Presidential American flags set in each front panel above the headlights flutter, not fly up at speed. The state's Special Squad cars to be driven at the front and rear of the motorcade are each fitted with a series of mirrors, giving them an almost 360 degree range of vision. Soon-to-be-Sir described it as Just like a Royal tour, only slightly exaggerated. The President's limousine's tyres are bullet-proofed and the boot contains two independent radio transmitters—one in reserve in case the main station fails. A secret service agent is secretly positioned between them in the boot in case either requires servicing. It's the cushiest job in the Service, but you must be of small stature to measure up. An ability to absorb unexpected bumps is born with them, not learnt.

Two bubble-tops were flown in, one each for Sydney and Melbourne. They are too heavy to make the trip up the Hume Highway via Albury. They'd be worse than the Army tanks on Dean Street on Anzac Day. And it would get awfully hot in the bubble-top with no shade except in the boot. Lady Bird would disappear as moisture. They'd all want to ride in the boot or with the top off and then what's the use?

Eighteen jet-black Lincolns, Cadillacs, Parisiennes and the odd Mercedes line up along the taxi rank outside the domestic terminal, engines revved by drivers every now and again to recheck that the engines are turning over and just for the heck of it. From time to time a black-suited chauffeur jumps out and pulls his hankie out and gives the windows the once-over. The bubble-top driver must have a huge hankie, and praises the foresight of Soon-to-be-Sir for his unique planning abilities which include the bowel habits of racing pigeons.

Two tabletop trucks have been seconded from private industry, painted black to fit in, and one each allotted to the White House press and local press. Their position in the parade is a secret—even, unfortunately, to the drivers. Movie and television cameras are mounted on the flat backs of the trucks. Cameramen guess as to their focus. A flying wedge of police motorcyclists has been training up and down the deserted streets of La Perouse. They are now so precise that the tip of their wedge might pierce even the side panel of the bubble-top.

On the tarmac the barrier is placed in exactly the same spot as when the Beatles arrived. Although no mass faintings or passings-out are expected, middle-aged women being made of sterner stuff than teenage girls, emergency bunks are available in the Qantas maintenance hangar. The rest of that space is a press facility with red telephones for overseas, black for locals, and the latest in rented desks, chairs and Telexes.

Soon-to-be-Sir promised this motorcade would have the elegant simplicity of a Royal progress. Ten government buses have been painted black and now quiver in anticipation as engines run steady to rush the press and other dignitaries from the airport to the Art Gallery for the Civic Reception. Soon-to-be-Sir rattles off orders to Mr Rod Murdoch of the Premier's Department, veteran of many Royal tours. Motorcades are black, people provide the colour. The white open limos might be all right for the tickertape parade for returning astronauts in New York, but they are in the same category as sportsmen, war heroes and lottery winners. Heads of state must stick to black. There are standards, god-damn it Murdoch!

Soon-to-be-Sir has read Dale Carnegie from cover to cover and back again. He is a whipper-snipper rapid-fire no-nonsense-but-the-best with the last fireworks for the Queen and eight Waratah Spring Festivals to his credit. He is in advertising when not working on pageants, bunting, placards, flags and slogans. Go Gay for LBJ is his own invention. He stops cynicism dead in its tracks. If anyone says it's corny, he says, Remember this: corn is awfully nourishing! He has one eye on the sword soon-to-be-placed on his shoulder after a lifetime of avoiding knives in his back and his other eye on the 200 million people who will be watching Sydney. We will make the whole of the world weekend press!

Soon-to-be-Sir's office has issued edicts to city offices to stay open today, Saturday, to allow staff and others to cheer the President and his motorcade down George Street in a New-York-style tickertape parade. The edict encouraged workers to tear up old yellow page phone books and even newspapers. Sydney downtown is not yet the financial and business centre to provide enough tickertape, so telephone books and newspapers have to do. The million yards of Go Gay for LBJ strips have unfortunately been distributed along the 14-mile route from the airport to the Art Gallery, where most buildings lining the way are single-storey houses. A roll of tape thrown from the window of a suburban house may not even reach the road, even if thrown by someone who fields at long on. Tickertape is meant to be thrown underarm.

If anyone is mad enough not to actually be there by the side of President Johnson's Way, George Street or the Art Gallery, then you can sit at home in your own armchair and watch the whole thing on television. It won't be as good as the real thing because colour TV hasn't yet come to Australia. If you don't like the coverage on Channel 9 you can get out of the armchair and turn the dial to Channel 7. If that isn't to your liking you can get out of the chair and change the setting to Channel 10 or Channel 2. Sydney has four channels and all of them are covering the President, live. (Strangely for a big country, America only has three channels, which all cover the tour. Two in colour and one in black and white, for the nostalgic.) If you are sick of the whole thing you'll have to turn the television off. Perhaps you could think about a device that might allow channel changing from an armchair. Maybe a long lead under the carpet, with a switch built into the armchair rest. Who knows.

I'm into the visit, live and real time in the Domain. This is history in the making. Television is for those who prefer history in the remaking. Moffitt has us all in a huddle near the wire mesh protecting the native shrubs. He runs up and down, corralling us like a sheepdog. Simmo and I look left and right for opportunities to get lost in the crowd.

Built in fits and starts at the turn of the century, the Art Gallery of New South Wales has six sandstone pillars at the entrance. Its builders carved on its sandstone façade the names of painters, sculptors and architects, names considered in the late 1890s to be men of lasting significance. Such was not always the case, but sandstone names are the devil to erase and their names may well live on if only in Sydney sandstone, famous for nothing else but their presence on the gallery façade, like honour boards at schools.

The Art Gallery building sits at the very end of Art Gallery Road. Sydney city planners are a simple no-nonsense lot. A large grassy area called the Domain surrounds it. The great advantage of choosing the Art Gallery is that dignitaries attending the reception can park their cars on the grass. Invitations have been sent from Soon-to-be-Sir's office to a broad spectrum of people in the top echelon to mingle with the Johnsons in the courtyard of the Art Gallery. Soon-to-be-Sir has read that Johnson is a man of the people. Surely only the top people, he thought. Ordinary top people have been plucked from the busy life of the city and deposited with their startled wives in the internal courtyard of the gallery. A cross-section of Sydney's citizens sip from special glasses imprinted with crossed US and Australian flags and nibble on asparagus fingers covered with grated Australian cheddar cheese on toasted bread soldiers. The lack of little boys' and girls' rooms is made up for by an impressive line of bottle-green Port-a-loos at the back of the Art Gallery where, if you push the tightly sprung fibreglass doors open just a bit, you can get the best views of Sydney Harbour anywhere on the foreshore.

Judges mix with financiers who rub shoulders with aldermen who stand by retailers and real estate tycoons and whitegoods manufacturers. A real slice of Sydney's top men-in-the-street, well, men in the street if they happen to be walking from their office to their waiting limo. An occasional sports hero, retired of course, and politicians from both sides of Parliament complete this snapshot of Sydney society. Soon-to-be-Sir must be thrilled with this informal gathering of ordinary top people done up to the nines or some such figure.

Outside, Simmo and I see our chance and grab the fish, carpe diem, hiding in a scrum of nuns swirling in a flickering pack for a better view. Once free of Moffitt and the length of his right cross and sneak uppercut, Simmo and I stick our boaters inside the thin wire mesh protecting the instant bushland, where they will surely be safe. We cover them with the heaped mulch gathered in the bag-catchers of Victa motor mowers that have gone up and down the Domain grasslands for the last week. You'd have thought they were playing a cricket test on it. Simmo pulls a new tie for each of us out of his sleeves like Mandrake and we pull the Windsor knots of our school ties apart with the ease with which Windsor knots tend to fall apart these days, like parachutes. Simmo has knocked off The Bike's dad's latest clip-on ties in the brilliant oranges and reds and yellows popular with David Jones front window dressers and former barbers who are now calling themselves hair stylists. Ever cool, Simmo pulls a pair of The Bike's dad's Ray-Bans for himself from his top pocket and a pair of black diamante wingtips for me. Mrs Bike will be as furious as I am. It's better than nothing. Barely.

Leaving Grantie and The Bike with the rest of the repeaters will throw Moffitt for sure. Even if he can't quite see us among the ebb and throng of boys, he believes the four of us stick together like sherpas on ropes. With our blue suits, boaterless heads, long pants and sunglasses we are on the lookout for Georgina and Katie and their peaceniks. There must be 20,000 people in front of the Art Gallery and, by a rule of thumb that has proved useful down the ages, half are women.

For the thousands outside the Art Gallery Soon-to-be-Sir has set up another forest of speaker boxes on giant poles, half a dozen at a time, hanging like handbags on hallstands. Nothing but the best to hear their masters' voices. The speaker boxes bellow what sounds like Tasting one two three but is an announcer testing with a juicy plum in his mouth for the great occasion.

On the gravel road outside the gallery a platoon of blue-suited constables in aviator glasses stand shoulder to shoulder with G-men in black Ray-Bans, dark suits and white shirts. All their armpits look as if they've been sprayed with Mortein that dried and got wet again, leaving whitish cloud-like wave patterns on their jackets. A long carpet of brown underfelt, courtesy of Waks Bros Carpets, rolls out of the mouth of the gallery entrance and hangs exhausted down the six steps to the gravel. Waiters and other workers walk into the Art Gallery on the best underfelt Sydney has to offer. This is a people's pageant and they are to be given the full underlay treatment. Carpet layers with mouthfuls of tacks and small hammers in their hands come to the rescue and quickly lay the red carpet over the underfelt, short six inches on either side but neatly tucked into the corners of the stone steps with pieces of pine covered in bent nails, giving some purchase to the tight carpet. Workers are ordered to use only the sides of the runway, and to walk carefully on the six-inch perimeters of underfelt.

The crowds on the lawns outside are as thick as on Macleay Street in front of the Sheraton Hotel when the Beatles came onto the balcony of their room and waved to us all in the street or on television, which I watched at Aunt Liberty's on weekend leave, sitting cross-legged in front of her Pye 21-inch. Uncle Liberty always purchased the latest products as he was in the industry, and a thick film of cellophane-like plastic stuck over the glass in front of the screen gave the broadcast a slightly colourised hue from certain angles in their loungeroom.

Two columns of cops with their holsters on one side
of their belt and batons on the other separate the
crowds of well-wishers from the unwell-wishers waving
handwritten placards and shouting obscenities like
Bloody Holt! and Damn Johnson! Aunt Liberty's ears
would turn blue if she could hear them. They are even
louder than the test broadcast from within the sandstone walls of the Art Gallery. Across the heads and
hats of supporters we can just make out the posters
and placards on sticks going up and down taller than
the tallest cop.

Mums and dads have brought young children from
as far afield as Katoomba in the Blue Mountains and
Newcastle in the north. Some families have packed
lunches into their Tupperware and brought Eskys to
stand on. Others stand on tippy-toes to glimpse the
groups of protesters mustered near the instant bush setting, unsettling the nervous wallabies and kangaroos
startled by their first visit to the New South Wales Art
Gallery. The instant bush is also nothing like they
remember from the outside or have heard about from
parents or other animals. The great bush certainly has
never heard shouts of Out now! and Fucking pigs! even
if a huge razorback were bearing down on them. A
canapé of carrots has been tastefully placed in the
upturned earth at the foot of the just-planted ghost
gums and eucalyptus. Koalas seek out the highest points
of these new trees, which give some shade and a view
over their wet noses, if only they could see. Simmo and

I weave in and out until we come to the no-man's-land blocking one group from the other.

* * *

In the meantime or roughly thereabouts, give or take a couple of minutes, Air Force One sweeps through what the pilot thinks are unusual cloud formations. Had he been standing on the ground he would not have been in a position to fly the President. However, he would have seen that a giant part of Sydney's Welcoming Committee's money has gone up in smoke. The skywriter's attempt to spell out the slogan All the way with LBJ has been blown away by high winds and smudged by unexpected real cloud puffs. Letters bump into each other over Sydney's midday skyline as if written with the side of a stick of chalk rather than its point. A chorus of tut-tuts and what-a-shames rises from the crowd gathered on the observation deck of the overseas terminal at Mascot Airport. They gasp as Air Force One bursts from the alphabet soup of clouds and running writing. Soon-to-be-Sir makes a mental note never to hire skywriters on cloudy or windy days again.

Many in the crowd arrived at the airport as early as 5 a.m. to catch a glimpse of the President and First Lady. Airport workers were astonished. The Beatles fans had not arrived this early, nor in fact had many of the workers who were supposed to start at 3 a.m.

The Committee has arranged two huge 60-foot building cranes to be driven onto the tarmac and a banner proclaiming Welcome Mr President to be hung between them. Airport security thought they were parked too close to the taxiway and ordered them moved. The crane drivers managed to move parallel for nearly fifty feet until one had to swerve suddenly to avoid a runaway child and the banner broke somewhere between Mr and President. Those aboard Air Force One must wonder what two cranes are doing parked in front of the terminal as the plane taxies down the tarmac.

A convoy of cars carrying the Governor and the Premier race towards the official dais, barely making it before Air Force One pulls alongside. Ten thousand hand-held flags wave excitedly as the President and his wife appear on the top of the steps. A marching band of state and Commonwealth police with two Thursday Islanders on secondment strike up The Yellow Rose of Texas or something fairly close to it. It was Lady Bird's favourite. Until now.

A thousand white plastic Texan ten-gallon hats have been promised to the first thousand kiddies to arrive at Mascot. Unfortunately Australian children have half-gallon heads but sensational ears which take the weight off the free hats in many cases. Most children are blinded by the hats and can't see the President's beaming smile. Then of course the President can't see theirs. The applause is spontaneous as soon as Premier Askin turns to the crowd and claps his hands and looks sternly at everyone. The Australian sense of poetry instantly takes charge and shouts of Enjoy your stay LBJ! and Hip hip hooray for LBJ! are heard.

The President slips down the steps and bear-hugs the Governor Sir Roden Cutler so hard that he is very nearly swept off his foot (having lost the other one during the war against the amputating unfree Frogs). He is almost 6 foot 6 inches tall and as he sways about some smart alec in the crowd yells Timber! Premier Askin steadies him and he limps across to the official dais with US Ambassador Ed Clark. He'd be a good foot larger if it wasn't for the machete-wielding Frogs. All the wives follow in a flock and fully frocked. It appears to onlookers that the President walks with a sympathetic limp just to make the Governor feel at ease. A six-year-old boy dressed in red stripes and spangled stars and a tall black striped stovepipe hat rushes out. The President takes his hand for a few steps like a man with a mouse on a leash.

Premier Askin extends a very warm and very hearty welcome from the oldest, most historical and largest city in Australia—Sydney! He assures the President that he knows he didn't come halfway round the world to listen to speeches. He then gives a lengthy impromptu speech reading from typed notes. Mrs Johnson has captured all Australian hearts, men and women alike! Demonstrators have been provided, he tells the President, to make him feel at home. But they are going to be drowned out, he says, fumbling for his glasses before reading on, by the loudest and most clarion-like noise in the world: the voice of the people. I know, Sir [nod to right], that you don't want to listen to me but want to meet the ordinary people of Sydney—and Mr President, they don't come more ordinary than the hundreds of thousands lined up along President Johnson Way to meet you and Mrs Johnson!

The President knows instinctively that the Premier will be a hard act to follow. He tells the crowds that if Ambassador Clark ever resigned, he could be the first applicant for the job. A smarty yells out Resign, Ed! from behind the police band. A large gust of wind almost instantly takes most of the white plastic Texan ten-gallon hats from the kiddies' heads and the President's notes from off the podium. Hats and papers twist along the tarmac like white wheels. High above the skyline, the skywriter's efforts look like the last words of a suicide note.

Soon-to-be-Sir bundles everyone into their limousines. Prime Minister Harold Holt keeps things running late as he takes advantage of the cosy atmosphere to shake as many hands as he can. The election is in full swing. The motorcade leaves the domestic portion of Mascot to drive down President Johnson's Way. Workers from an airline company start stitching the torn banner together with 10 lb fishing line. It might be ready for the President's departure.

Demo

Georgina always stands out in a crowd even though she is a little over 5 feet. Simmo has a word for it: boobs. No, just joking. Charisma. She certainly has it, and whenever I'm with her and a little bit rubs off I grow about half a foot, though in a very different direction. She is, as Dad says, generously proportioned. She has a placard hammered onto a plank of wood in her hands high above her head. It reads Is it Gay in Vietnam? Katie towers over her but seems somehow smaller. She holds a placard in front of her like a shield. In Katie's own hand it reads Stop the War. Georgina has all the talent in that friendship.

Georgina and Katie are surrounded by hundreds of other student protesters directing their anger and voices at the line of police officers forming a rigid cordon around the Art Gallery entrance and fanning out down the stone steps onto the gravel roadway. The cops have locked arms to prevent enthusiasts and demonstrators alike from rushing into the stream of dignitaries mounting the steps for the reception. The protesters are naturally on the left. Simmo and I don't belong to a political party but any organisation with the word 'party' in it we'll give a go.

Cars are piling up and disgorging those dubbed Mr and Mrs Sydney for the day by Soon-to-be-Sir Asher Joel. Senior judges, business leaders, academics, diplomats, architects and cabinet ministers, all with their wives in the latest French fashions from the top floor of David Jones department store and fox furs, ideal for Sydney's spring heatwaves. These women are definitely part of the stole generation. All the great churches are represented by purple-robed archbishops and priests. Soon-to-be-Sir's Committee has invited a solitary Aboriginal representative, a Mr Charles Perkins. It was noted he was from the exclusive suburb of Vaucluse.

On one side of the steps protesters cry out abuse and outrage. On the other side, cheers for the people's representatives. I tell Simmo we are on the wrong side and we duck under the locked arms of two policemen and run across the pavement between dismayed dignitaries to join the girls. Mounted police patrol between the slow-moving motor vehicles on the outlook for the first hint of trouble. Is that a rhetorical question? I shout, pointing at her sign, to a surprised Georgina. No but yours was. It's hard to tell if she's pleased to see us but I detect a softening in the way that she shouts 1-2-3-4 we don't want your fucking war.

She looks good enough to eat. She has her sunglasses pushed up over her bangs on top of her forehead. Her red-lipsticked mouth makes moving ovals as she screams obscenities to the top men holding their wives' hands and leading them up the stairs. Every time she says fuck I nearly cream myself. Swearwords can be so erotic in the right hands. The ladies hold their long dresses with the other hand lest they trip. Occasionally they wave to the crowd on the right. State receptions are a bit like going to Mass. Ladies have to wear hats. Orthodox Jewish married ladies have to wear hats so that only their husbands can ogle their hair. Catholic ladies must wear hats in church lest it tempt the priest to run his white communion fingers through their locks. At state receptions for US Presidents it is a bit of both. US Presidents have a keen eye for the ladies and their hair, and Sydney dignitaries don't like other people perving on or messing with their missus's curls.

Now that Simmo and I are with the protesters we can feel the anger welling up within us. Our faces redden with the rage and grow on fire. We have our sunglasses on and our wide bright ties so we can feel the righteous fury that going incognito gives those not so brave. My first Out now! can hardly be heard by myself. Only nearby lip readers could make any sense of my preliminary protests. But Georgina's proud look at me and the comfort of the crowd soon have me swearing and cursing at the file of fine guests and the police force that keeps us from them. Georgina gives me a peck with tongue on my fired-up cheek. I wish I had done a year of geography so that I'd know where Vietnam is. But wherever it is, I shout Out now! at the top of my voice with more guts than was ever put into a Double Waverley at the footy. Protesting makes you horny. Simmo says even Katie is beginning to look cute. We're all using swearwords. It's an orgy of swearwords. Not just f's but c's too.

I keep an eye out of the side of my diamantes for Brother Moffitt. The church is for the war because the communists don't believe in God and their women are not only hatless heathens but are fighting side by side with their men against the Catholic South Vietnamese. You wouldn't find Catholics priests dousing themselves with metho and going up in smoke. It's Unchristian. They're more likely to be drinking it.

The police keep pushing back so that we're crushed against each other. That is mighty fine with me because I'm pushed flat against Georgina, so close that I can smell the 4711 and talc rising from her squeezed body. I feel the familiar throb of lover's balls beginning to ache in my David Jones spare pair of pants, given away with each complete school uniform purchased. Behind us is a male student with a sign that is really a sight-testing eye chart. He is perhaps Sydney's first yippie and yet to find a group where he really belongs. Police officers pretend they understand its random letters and push him over. Fancy printing that in public.

* * *

Soon-to-be-Sir smiles sweetly with self-satisfaction as the motorcade slowly snakes along Ross Smith Avenue leaving Mascot airport. Things are going swimmingly. People are lined up along President Johnson's Way née King Street as far as the eye can see over the chauffeur's shoulders. They are two or three thick in places. He can see the bubble-top just one car ahead and the back of the President's huge head and the black bird's nest of hair atop Lady Bird. Not an unpleasantry to be seen.

Youth clubs and Returned Services League bands play various themes from great wars and films. Six black-suited bodyguards run alongside the bubble-top, jumping from time to time onto the running boards. You have to get out of bed early to outfox Soon-to-be-Sir in the promotions and parades department.

President Johnson's Way was advertised as going along Anzac Parade. The new University of New South Wales is plum in the middle, along about half a mile of Anzac Parade. Soon-to-be-Sir has heard on the grapevine that the layabout students have planned a protest outside their grounds and paint bombs were being prepared in the ghostly red and black of the Vietcong. The Welcoming Committee have spies planted everywhere. Cunningly, the committee secretly alerted the lead motorbikes and cars to avoid the university and to cut down Barker Street in Kensington, through

Houston Road and along Doncaster Avenue behind the university. Students are left in their dirty clothes and hair, holding their paint bombs in plastic bags, looking down President Johnson Way towards the airport long after the motorcade has ducked back onto Anzac Parade and is speeding towards the waiting city.

On the steps of the Town Hall the Lord Mayor, Alderman Armstrong, and his entire council stand on their toes to look as tall as possible. Swarms of shoppers jam George Street in front of the lucky aldermen, unable to move or wave the free flags clasped tightly against their thighs by the throng. Town Hall station below keeps throwing up free passengers from the country. People from Bourke and Temora in far west New South Wales are stranded on the platform in the underground holding red white and blue balloons and handfuls of confetti.

At Queens Square volunteer gardeners snip the shoulders of the floral carpet. Birdmen hush the thousand starving pigeons that cry out for breadcrumbs. Two thousand nuns from all over New South Wales gather at Taylor Square under the great banner saying The Eyes of Sydney Are Upon You. A thousand voices of the Mormon Tabernacle male choir rehearse The Battle Hymn of the Republic at the intersection of Oxford and College streets. Those lucky enough to get access to the roofs along Oxford Street start throwing ribbons of tickertape and many throw rolls of fresh toilet paper long before the motorcade is within sight.

A young man in dark glasses and saffron robes runs up and down in front of the War Memorial with a petrol can, threatening to set himself alight. Passers-by flick their cigarettes at him. There has been a rash of self-immolations among Buddhist monks in Asia recently and some Australians are anxious not to be left behind. This young man is taking no chances and has filled the petrol can with water, with which he douses himself regularly. A fireman with an extinguisher at his side runs with him in case called upon. Soon-to-be-Sir has factored in even the bizarre.

Windows in skyscrapers are all open and papers, flags, balloons and anything to hand flutters out like thick rain. Security men patrol the streets on the look-out for the ratbag element. In the instant bush a koala has to be poked in the behind as he tries to climb down the transplanted gum tree. The cold end of a police baton has him skimming back up the bark. The roar of the crowds and the hovering helicopters are stirring up the animals inside the perimeter. The set of twin albino wallabies, a gift from Sir and Lady Askin to the Johnsons, crap in fear in their cages under the eaves of the northern side of the Art Gallery. The wind on Sydney Harbour picks up quickly and hundreds of pleasure craft jog in place on the choppy waters outside the imaginary no-go zone where only the *Captain Phillip* can cruise.

Soon-to-be-Sir hears on his walkie-talkie the Police Commissioner's estimate of the crowd in the city: one million. He punches his fist in the air, hitting the roof of the limo and grazing a knuckle. He doesn't feel it at all in the excitement. He sits smiling in the back of his limousine while the President makes another unscheduled stop to hand out souvenir LBJ ballpoints and to use the bullhorn to greet the baffled but proud Greek greengrocers at a corner in Kingsgrove. They keep the biros tucked neatly behind their ears for days, flourishing them to shoppers while writing the weight of tomatoes on brown paper bags.

The Police Commissioner has positioned himself at Taylor Square where President Johnson's Way doglegs suddenly to the left into what was formerly Oxford Street. He is worried about the number of bearded young men and bra-less young women gathered on the corner. The spearhead of police motorcyclists is heading towards him followed by the convoy of black limousines, the bubble-top and black buses and lorries. He quickly estimates there are more people in Taylor Square alone than at last year's footy final without using any of his fingers. Streams of toilet paper, confetti and tickertape fall on the heads of his officers lined up to keep the crowds in place.

Commissioner Norm Allen is a cool head in time of trouble. He is very proud of the way he handled the Wally Melish siege. Wally had held police at bay with a shotgun for days, keeping his girlfriend hostage. The Commissioner had defused the whole thing by acting as best man while Wally and his hostage married in a civil wedding ceremony. He is a humble man with much to be humble about. He had stopped the Melish affair from turning into a fiasco. But he can smell panic as his young officers stumble forward under the surging weight of people on the footpaths behind them. The G-men are of absolutely no use in crowd control. The Commissioner looks down Oxford Street towards the city. It is alive with bits of paper. He can't see past his own very bulbous nose. He's pulled officers into Sydney from all over the state but he now feels there might not be enough. He can't make out what the placards the bearded students are holding say without his glasses but he knows it isn't friendly greetings. What worries him further are the black streamers and bomb-shaped balloons some of the protesters throw onto the road. The G-men might mistake them for the real thing.

The 50 tons of tickertape and cut-up paper hit the air as soon as the motorbikes head down Oxford Street. The cyclists have to stop every yard to take the paper off their necks and arms. The motorcade begins to slow to a crawl. The barricade finally bursts open and dozens of protesters run in front of limousines and lie down flat on the road. Premier Askin shouts to his driver to Ride over the bastards! Soon-to-be-Sir tugs at his sleeve and says that that might be misconstrued. There are womenfolk amongst them he cries. There are no women fighting with the allies in Vietnam. Only the enemy stoops so low. The Commissioner lends a hand, grabbing the sockless ankles of a prone student and ups-a-daisy throwing him on the count of three back into the crowd with two of his officers holding an arm each.

The motorcade is stop–start all the way down Oxford Street as police throw protesters off the roadway only to have them scurry back. The women fight as hard as the men. The Commissioner has never seen anything like it. Soon-to-be-Sir sticks his head out the side window but can't see far because of the paper hailing down from the rooftops and awnings. The President's bubble-top has come to a complete stop outside Zink's Tailors and Gentlemen's Outfitters. Rufus Youngblood and five others mount the running boards. The President and Lady Bird can't see out and no one in the crowd can see in, only now and then a glimpse of his head and her hair.

Police start to arrest the road-sitters and cuff them, sometimes around the ears. Many police officers lose their caps in the melee and children run off with them tucked under their arms. Soon-to-be-Sir orders the Commissioner to get things moving out in front. Speed up, speed up! he barks into his walkie-talkie. It's all right for some thinks the Commissioner, flinging another bearded student into the back of a paddy wagon.

Inside the bubble-top the President is sweating like a pig. Lady Bird's beautiful hair is draining down her forehead. The President can hardly breathe. He sees the occasional banner, Butcher Bird, We Mourn Our

Boys, Out Now!, Stop the War. It's hotter than Hades, he tells his driver. The bubble-top has stopped moving. The White House on Wheels has lost its air conditioning. Inside the bulletproof glass and three-inch steel padding with the most up-to-date radio communications ever produced, the President and his wife are slowly melting away. The air conditioning has clogged up with tickertape and confetti. The driver jumps out and pulls yards and yards of it out of the grille, handful after handful, as if unpacking a huge present. He jumps back in and still the air conditioning won't work. The slickest vehicle in the world has been brought to its knees by Soon-to-be-Sir's 50 tons of tickertape. Then the million-dollar limousine's engine stops dead as confetti and tape and paper jam it.

The Commissioner can see immediately what has happened and alerts Soon-to-be-Sir by walkie-talkie. The Premier says the Johnsons can get in with him. Soon-to-be-Sir knows that it would be a bit of a squeeze with the lanky Texan and her hair and orders another limousine immediately. All the state's fleet is in the motorcade but there is a Commonwealth car available that is usually used for state funerals. It has black-tinted windows and a two-way radio with AM and FM facilities.

The protesters are encouraged by the motorcade's sudden stall, and believing it is their doing they throw themselves even more vigorously into the fray. The Commissioner calls for reinforcements. Protesters shout

1-2-3-4 we don't want your fucking war! into the President's vulnerable stalled bubble-top. You can hardly hear The Yellow Rose of Texas being sung by the thousand voices of young Mormons at Hyde Park corner. The eighteen limousines are bumper-to-bumper, choked to a stop along Oxford Street. A riot threatens. The Premier wonders if his appointment of Soon-to-be-Sir was ill conceived. American cars. We should have stuck with the Holdens. They can put a monkey in space but can't get a car down Oxford Street. What else can go wrong?

* * *

You couldn't have fitted another dignitary or his wife into the Art Gallery with a crowbar. We jeer them all as they mount the steps, walk past admiring the instant bush and bushlife, and grimly but determinedly enter the front doors. Georgina has let me hold her hand and after about half an hour it is getting a bit sweaty but I don't want to let go. It's awkward for her being so small. She has to bend her elbow up and I sort of stoop a few inches, making it totally uncomfortable for both of us. But once I have her hand I don't want to give it up. The Brothers frown upon the holding of hands, claiming it would lead further up the arm and down the body. I was never much at holding hands. They just leak sweat and when I finally get my hand back to myself it looks like a railroad map of inner

Sydney stockyards. Georgina has extraordinarily long white fingers for someone so short.

All this contact is causing me no end of discomfort in the balls area. It is a dull hard throb. I bend over to kiss her lips but she keeps on shouting Out now! even though my lips are over hers. It's hard to get something going under these conditions. All I can do is shout Out now! back in sync into her mouth. The police try to move us off the steps but we push back. Simmo and Katie are getting close, I can tell. It's just something in the way he has his hand down the back of her shirt and half way up the front. How long has this been going on? He winks under his Ray-Bans.

There won't be an oyster with a pearl left in the world because millions of them are hung around the necks, several times with some, of the ladies inside the Art Gallery. Pearls are the pendants of choice for the stole generation. They try to pet the kangaroos and wallabies but the animals are hopping furiously around, nervous with the noise. Only the echidna stands still, wistfully waiting to be patted by a gloved hand or two. The white cockatoos in the potted ghost gums screech and try to fly, only to realise their legs have been tied to the branches with string. The gallery buzzes with excitement. It seems like hours since they arrived to be greeted by waiters with asparagus fingers and the finest Australian sherry, available in sweet or dry.

* * *

In the back seat of his Ford Parisienne, Soon-to-be-Sir Asher Joel would have been beside himself except that would have placed him fairly and squarely on the Premier's considerable lap. Mr Askin wouldn't have taken kindly to that. He isn't a giddyup kind of man. The entire motorcade waits with engines running until the black Commonwealth funeral car makes its way along Oxford Street and comes to a halt alongside the big bubble-top. The President bounds out of the heat haze inside the bubble-top, takes in a few heady gulps of air and howdies the crowd, handing out a few more ballpoints to the lucky. Lady Bird is escorted into the new car and waits for her husband to join her.

At Queens Square the pigeon handlers prepare their birds. Scores of marching girls and drum majorettes practise their moves to themselves in small steps. The Aldermen are getting restless outside the Town Hall. Many are of an age where they can't wait in their seats for Intermission. Finally everybody, including the President with his bullhorn between his legs, is ready to start the motorcade up again, down Oxford and Liverpool streets and then past the Town Hall, Queens Square and on to the Art Gallery. Almost at once the President notices that he can't see out through the windows of the new car. From two large cars behind, Soon-to-be-Sir sees that you can't see in either. After all the planning and all the late-night meetings of the Welcoming Committee, it has come to this. The President is to drive through the entire city reception in a blackened car, unseen and unseeing, while a million people by the Commissioner's estimate, give or take a few fingers, wave blind as bats. The whole parade is quickly becoming a charade. It is way behind time and Soon-to-be-Sir feels the sword not on his shoulder but drifting into the blades of his back, held by the angry citizens of Sydney. He shouts into his walkie-talkie to drive at maximum speed. Get it over quick. Maybe no one will notice.

If it wasn't for the fact that most of the city's traffic cops are up the front of the motorcade clearing a path, they could have made a fortune booking the limos for speeding through the city. Most of the million-by-the-Commissioner's-estimate see only a black blur as the motorcade snakes at top speed down Liverpool Street and along George Street, past the Town Hall steps. The aldermen hardly have time to raise their hands before the cars speed past. Country children, lined up for hours, burst into tears. Loud booing breaks out in the ranks. The President throws his hat through the black window he manages to unwind outside the Town Hall and a lucky female pounces on it. People cheer at any black car, peering in only to see Soon-to-be-Sir or some dignitary they couldn't give a hoot about. Mothers and fathers curse the hide of the government who dragged us in for nothing. Flags are thrown into the gutters in disgust. It's a swindle!

The chief pigeon fancier has no idea which car Lady Bird is travelling in and long after she has passed by he runs along the cages tied up at Queens Square and releases the starving pigeons into the air. They burst from their seedless cages in an explosion of grey and purple feathers. As it turns out, Soon-to-be-Sir needn't have worried about the bubble-top but the damage is done and the thousand pigeons barely reach the tree-tops before falling out of the sky like feathered hailstones from lack of food. Three days off the seed was too much, and the birds struggle to stay in the air before falling in thuds at the feet of the stunned bystanders. A thousand pigeons lying stunned and twitching on the footpath brings all the excitement very much down to earth.

The marching girls and drum majorettes stand still as the motorcade takes them completely by surprise. The floral tribute is trampled into mulch as the crowd runs across it to follow the cars. The lucky ones watch it all on television. Well over a million, estimates the Commissioner when asked the number of viewers. He rounds everything off to the nearest million.

The revving of bikes and limos drowns out much of the booing that breaks out when the motorcade finally pulls up in front of the Art Gallery steps. Hundreds of demonstrators run from Hyde Park to the Art Gallery to join their compatriots in arms. Brother Moffitt has done his sums and Simmo points him out as he jumps up and down in the crowd looking for us. He bounces like a red-headed buoy in all directions. He'll murder us if he sees us. For sure. We are saved by the arrival of other protesters, pressing the police line to bursting from behind. Suddenly a group breaks through, trampling the waratahs and flannel flowers underfoot, sending press, police and kangaroos scurrying in all directions. The instant bush is debushed in an instant. Ghost gums fall to the ground, sending koalas running off to nearby telegraph poles for a perch. Wallabies and roos lose their cool in the stream of protesters. The wire mesh falls down and curls up like burning paper.

Inside the Art Gallery, the welcoming speeches are beginning. Prime Minister Harold Holt says Australia is prepared to vigorously fight aggression wherever it rears its head. The Premier Mr Askin tells the gathering that they are standing on the exact spot, almost, where the Australian nation was born 188 years ago. Mr Charles Perkins must be blushing under his Aboriginal skin. The American Ambassador rips the seat out of his pants and wears his ten-gallon hat over the tear. The President is obviously getting tired because he thanks Mr Mayor (referring to the Premier), compliments Lady Bolte (nodding to Mrs Askin), and speaks highly of the newspaper the *Sydney Morning World*. The hooting outside drowns his speech out. As the motorcade begins to leave for Circular Quay, Soon-to-be-Sir pales at the tattered mess of instant bush. St John's Ambulance men rush to the bottom of a telegraph pole where a koala has fallen after electrocuting itself on the wire. They baulk at mouth to mouth with a nose as wet as a koala's.

On board the *Captain Phillip* the President, the Premier, the Governor and the Ambassador lunch with their wives. The men admire the bikini-clad sun worshippers on the thousand pleasure craft floating outside the no-go zone. The ladies exchange gifts and sip on Australian wines in special sandblasted glasses. LBJ changes into his powder blue ranch suit with epaulettes below deck and emerges to a roar from the riggers hanging off the Opera House on safety ropes. At Hoyts theatre on George Street a hundred usherettes in uniform stand to attention on the awning outside, torches tucked up their right arms, oblivious to the fact that the motorcade passed by an hour earlier. As a mark of respect the pictures are put back two hours.

Our boaters are covered by a half-ton of mud and completely beyond repair. Simmo and I slip our school ties back on and bob up with the other repeaters behind Brother Moffitt's back near the bus.

Thirteen men and two women appear in Central Court on charges relating to the Art Gallery on Monday morning. Most are charged with offensive language, traffic obstruction or hindering police. A union official is charged with placing himself in a public place to beg alms and another gets four months for vagrancy. Never go to a demo without money in your pocket.

Seven Sleeps

Air Force One wings its way to Manila with the albino wallabies bedded down up the back under deep anaesthetic. They are very much out of bounds by the time they arrive at the Manila Peace Conference.

You could have knocked me down with a feather when Simmo says we only have seven sleeps before the leaving certificate exams start. None of us has swatted anything but flies for the whole year, and now it's over. The cruellest thing of all is that the state government has decided to bring in daylight saving, and everyone has to turn their watches forward an hour, and heaven help those with sundials. There's nothing wrong with the concept except that it takes an hour from you at exam time, when it's really needed because you've left everything to the last moment, and then they give you back the hour at the beginning of the next year, when you don't need it and you've got all the time in the

132

world plus an extra hour. Simmo says it's daylight rob-
bery. What if you die before next March? Grantie feels
it's against nature and will lead to flooding. Simmo
says it's the thin end of the wedge. It's an hour this
year, two hours next year, and before you know it
you're going back to bed after breakfast.

Mein Furner says it'll be lights out in five minutes
so we'd better shake a leg if we want to fit in a quick
decade of the rosary. Simmo and I roll our eyes. Sure.
It's been a long day protesting and heckling the
President but I'm not too tired to borrow The Bike's
Atlas of the World to see where Vietnam is. I would-
n't want the US to get out of there if it's too close to
Australia. It's miles away, thank God. On the other
hand, it seems that the Unchristian Brothers of Albury
might have had a point with the yellow chalk arrows
coming down the blackboard. The domino theory is
the yellow peril played with plastic pieces.

Mein Furner flicks the lights off and I lie in bed
waiting for my eyes to adjust to the dark. Moonlight
bounces into the dorm through the quadrangle windows off the immaculately white back of Our Lady of
the Mount. The dorm glows in a light the colour of
pingpong balls. It would be a sacrilege to be touching
and taking advantage of yourself in full view of Our
Lady, so I turn over the other way and slowly hump
my hand. The repeaters' dormitory after lights out on
a Saturday night is not so much filled with your coming
of age, but more your age of coming.

While most are dreaming and creaming of Little Pattie, I remain faithful to Georgina in the firm fold of my five fingers. Christine Keeler on her formica chair remains crushed between the kapok mattress and the springs. Even looking at the magazine would make me feel guilty about Georgina. But sometimes when I kiss Georgina I think of Christine Keeler. Catholics get the guilts coming and going. If you do it once you may as well go the whole hog and do it over and over, and start again after confession. Not that I believe in that shit any more, but it doesn't stop you feeling guilty about not believing any more. It's a vicious circle. If they get you by seven they have you until at least seventeen. It's pre-coital depression.

Mein Furner leaves his door open a crack in case any boy feels during the night that he needs to talk things over. Sure thing.

In the immaculate moonlight I can see a couple of boys on the other side of the dorm get up and tiptoe to the windows. They put their forearms through the open window and pull the bottom frame down hard on the underside until the blood stops running. The hand becomes numb and they rush back to their beds where their hands will feel completely dead and unconnected to their own bodies, but fleshy, like someone else. Your hand feels like it's gone to sleep. So humping your numb hand is unarmed combat with yourself. It's committing necrophilia with yourself. It isn't my thing. If they don't come quickly they rush up to the window again and numb their hand some more. We think numb is dumb. You can't hold a cigarette in your hand afterwards. I like the feel of life in my hand, and vice versa. Self-love involves a bit of give and take on both sides.

In the morning the moans of boys tearing their willies off dried sheets is more than I can stand. It's much better to catch it in your hand and wipe it into the blanket. Waverley College grey wool army blankets were made for sperm. You could start a population explosion by putting the boarding school laundry into the city's water supply. The Brothers say we'll all go blind if we keep doing it. It'll probably be called carpal tunnel vision syndrome or something. Contrary to the teaching, my eyesight is actually getting better.

Moscow Zoo lent its giant panda An-An to London Zoo last year in order to mate with Chi-Chi. It's now been over a year and nothing has happened. Zoologists fear they will not hear the pitter-patter of little pandas. I know how they feel. It's been a couple of months with Georgina and I'm beginning to feel like An-An or Chi-Chi or whichever was which. They both sound like pansies. Whenever I think of the exams coming up my stomach turns over like a washing machine. But if I think of Georgina my stomach turns like a spin dryer, so much so that I have to go to the toilet for much of the hour before I'm supposed to meet her. It's undeniable. I'm in love. A virgin in love with a vamp.

Something's got to give. The irresistible force in love with the immovable object of his affections.

* * *

Simmo complains that his hands are too small to write everything on them he needs to know for English Literature on Monday. I tell him to undo his sleeve button and work up his forearm. He started too early, and sweat and showers rub out his precious crib notes. He has to start all over again. His wooden rulers are allotted a subject each. Six subjects means six rulers. He has *Henry V* down to three inches covering most of the major themes and characters. There is an inch or two of poems and a couple of inches for the essays of Charles Lamb. He has enough ruler left to cover great Australian writers, if we'd studied them. The history of the world between World War I and World War II is completely covered in 12 inches. It's in code and on one side only. You wouldn't want to mix those rulers up, I tell him. He's a walking Enigma Machine. He explains it isn't cheating because in real life you're allowed to have a ruler with stuff written on it. Prime Ministers don't have to memorise their speeches. Examinations are so artificial.

The leaving certificate is a public examination and the state hires the keenest eyes in the country to look out for tricks like rulers, notes in your socks and hieroglyphics on your hand. The type of person who supervises the examinations also scrutineers the elections. You can't pull the wool over their eyes. Usually because they are asleep on their chairs. They have nothing on the Unchristian Brothers, who could spot a cheat from the next room with the door closed and who have eyes in the backs of their heads.

Around exam time you'd expect the Dux of College to be one of the most popular boys ever in the class. Kids would suck up to him to borrow or copy his study notes in order to catch up. However, I've been so slack this year that my entire work and preparation is one blank page. Everyone knows it, and except for a question or two don't bother even asking. We're all in the same race, a field of Bernboroughs with no front runners except maybe Roger Ng. He keeps his notes in Chinese, much to Simmo's surprise when he pinched them one night to copy. Simmo put them back, saying he wasn't a good judge of characters anyway. He's always cracking us up with stuff like that. He's full of contradictions, like he speaks fluent Latin but swears like a shearer with the shakes. Dominus Fucking Vobiscum.

When Mein Furner reads out the lucky letter-getters at dinner, most of the repeaters get cards from their family wishing them Good luck or God speed or Don't come home if you fail. In the first few years I spent at Waverley College Captain Jack Saunders (retired) sent a damp ten shilling note with a message written on the banknote itself every year for my birthday. The note would be crumpled and moist and looked as if it came from the very bottom of his trouser pocket. It smelt of wet tobacco with a hint of urine. I didn't mind because I knew it really came from the middle of his heart. But he's tailed off in the last couple of years, probably spending it on beer at Dad's pub—so I'm getting it indirectly. I haven't heard a word from home since Mum came to Speech Night and embarrassed me almost to death. I'd hoped for a letter at least but don't get a word. Simmo gets a telegram with one word: Goodluckmumanddad. His family have connections high up in the local post office and they got a sweetheart deal, paying for just one word.

* * *

Not only has Askin brought in daylight saving, but it feels as though the world is spinning much quicker than it used to. It's as if everyone on the other side of the earth is running on the spot, all in unison, like circus performers on giant balls, causing the entire world to spin so fast that preparation for the exams seems impossible. Hours pass like minutes and minutes like seconds and seconds in a flash. There isn't enough time to read the crib notes of *Henry V* let alone the whole bloody book. We prepare for exams as we always have, the Brothers way. We write out lines, time and again, hundreds of times, until we know it off by heart. If you want to avoid a poem's true meaning try writing it out fifty times. You may learn the words but you miss the spaces in between.

A sense of panic seizes the repeating year. The night cries in the dorm after lights out are replaced by the murmur of lips reciting Shakespeare or the causes of World War I at 100 miles an hour. We'd heard that soldiers on the battlefield could go for months without thinking about sex or even getting a fat in the morning. The repeaters have their hands full of pens and pencils with no time to worry about putting them elsewhere. Simmo is making some last-minute notes on his calf, upside down, just below the sock line. He's beginning to look like the Tattooed Man from Sideshow Alley. He skips showers in the morning.

In the last week before exams we all go to morning Mass in the chapel, and communion rates go through the roof. It's a combination of not interfering with yourself, which leaves you remarkably in a state of grace, and hoping to get a leg up from God by a late rally of prayer. There's nothing like a public final exam, especially in a repeating year, to stir the fading faith back to life. If only God lets us pass, with Honours preferably, we'll go to Mass every Sunday and Holy Day of Obligation, starve in Lent and cut out well cut down the fiddling with the wedding tackle. We find the gift of faith like passengers in an out of control aeroplane in a thunderstorm. We make promises impossible to keep. Grantie crosses his heart and promises he'll join the priesthood. I tell him he'd be better off crossing his fingers.

We take communion every morning like it's brain food. Rosary beads and scapulars appear like magic from the bottom of luggage packed by our mums. The Little Sisters of the Rich up the road make a packet in holy cards. The repeating year is the last chance for most. Next year there'll be no more leaving certificates. The Wyndham Scheme has no places for leaving certificate students. These exams are no dress rehearsal for life. They are the real thing. If you fuck up, even the Unchristian Brothers won't take you in for training. You'll be out on the streets without your leaving certificate like an exile without a passport. Aunties around the state, from Bronte to Bourke, light long candles for St Teresa's intercession with God to top up our marks.

I on the other hand have nothing to lose. I already have a Commonwealth Scholarship to study medicine next year so despite the tension I'm confident enough to piss off after class down to Charing Cross to share a milkshake and a kiss and a cuddle or maybe more with Georgina.

Love is not a thief in the night who burgles your heart while you sleep. Love is an embezzler who takes a bit of it at a time, just enough so that you don't miss it, but slowly and steadily taking what's yours until one day you realise you don't have any more and in front of you the embezzler smiles with her pockets full to overflowing with those parts of you which are the best you have to give. If given a chance, you would have handed them over, but love must move under-handedly and build a secret trove of you before you realise that your pockets and chest cavity have been picked. There is just a heart-shaped hole. So it is with Georgina. In spades.

In the last week before the exams I fall helplessly in love with Georgina and hopelessly behind in my stud-ies. In Theo's Hot Chips and Sandwiches and on the grassy slopes of Queens Park we gaze into each other's eyes and graze on each other's lips and fingertips. During the protest outside the Art Gallery I saw a spirit in her I had never sensed before and a side of her I wanted to see more of—her backside. Just kidding. It isn't only skin but all else within. It's all perfect and I want her, but most of all I don't want anyone else to have her. The thought of losing her is worse than the prospect of failing the exams. The thought that some other boy with strong brown hands and perfect hair might one day be kissing her, and her him, and maybe even fucking her, makes my skin crawl. My stomach churns and my balls withdraw into my body as if I had walked into the cold sea. I am totally possessed by her, I am totally possessive of her. She is the object of my obsession. When you love one, you love everyone.

Love makes imperfections perfect. Georgina's large nose has become for me the perfect nose. I worship the bump on the bridge before the skin spreadeagles into two large fine nostrils. I cover it in kisses. It needs many. Her freckles are perfectly set, like diamonds in a necklace or stars in the sky, exactly in the right place, where they ought to be. I close my mind's eyes to the tanned bikinied beach girls, glistening in Johnson & Johnson's baby oil by the handful, of my previous fantasy life and grow quickly to realise that I love only her white ample skin, thick across her bottom and thighs as it ought to be and exactly the way I would make it myself if I had the gift. That's what love does to you. And more than that, she is herself and full of you, and you are you and full of her.

I walk on air. I could walk on water. There is significance in everything, the number of leaves in a tree, the angle of shadows on the street, clouds in the sky, the alignment of our freckles along our arms and across our backs when joined with a black pen marker to make symbols of substance.

In a rush I ask her to come to Albury for a week after school finishes. She'd love to. We kiss and tongue like cobras on heat. Georgina puts her hand up inside my dirty T-shirt and tickles my nipples. I think I'll explode. When I try to do the same to her, she gently brushes my hand off her Maidenform. No tit for tat? I ask. Later. That's an eternity. She says, Whichever comes first.

I understand. I understand everything. I understand why Dad loves Mum despite everything. Later can't come quickly enough.

But first I need to brush up a bit on lover's lingo. Between Modern History and Maths I swot for the right words. Between Latin and Chemistry I think of the right moves and during Physics I can't get my mind off her and the cool purring way she said Later. I know later is sooner than later. Later will soon be now and then instead of being imagined it will be a memory. I long for the memory even more than the thing itself. Once it's a memory I can turn it over and over on its side and study it like a specimen. It would be a certain shape and size and feel. Life is lived forwards. It is understood backwards.

Mum

Dr Tooth feels that Mum is not quite at her best, so he orders three ECTs. At Kenmore Hospital, little anaesthetic is given with the procedure. The pain of the current going through the body is initially absorbed in the shock. The prospect of ECT and its certain pain and shaking is the worst. The hospital employs local men of strength from nearby Goulburn. They alternate between jobs at Goulburn Maximum Security Gaol as prison guards and as assistants to subduing patients for ECT procedures.

No one is exactly sure why a large voltage of electricity passing through your head helps people with depression, but it appears to. It would be years before doctors came to learn that the patients could be put under anaesthetic to avoid the gruelling pain and still receive the mysterious benefits. In 1966, ECT therapy is a matter of trial and terror.

Exams

Simmo calls the Brothers creatures of habits. And so they are. Old Macdonald has them all lined up at assembly to wish the repeaters all the best in the exams, which are starting in the Great Hall at St Charles down the road. Many schools have great halls, even if they are no bigger than a kitchen. The senior school are all out in the quadrangle. The repeaters have cribs, books and papers in their hands, constantly checking and reciting lists as they read. We check our watches to see if somehow we might have got back the hour the state stole from us.

Old Macdonald gives us his blessing and asks the whole school to recite a Hail Mary for us, which takes forever and probably costs valuable swotting time. He revs us up with the We are Catholics speech, in a public examination, and we must do better than the public dogs. I giggle when he says our hard year's work will finally be paying off, but no one else does. They are as pale as ghosts. Old Macdonald says Once more unto the benches dear boys, which sounds vaguely familiar but I can't place it as I'm trying to keep *Henry V, The Rime of the Ancient Mariner* and the entire work of Charles Lamb in my head.

The key to exams for the Brothers is rote. Rote is the result of lines. Lines are what to write time and time again until you know it by heart. If you know spelling by heart, it really doesn't matter if you understand it or not. Rote is right.

Simmo shows me his hands. His palms are the colour of toilet Blue Duck. Old Macdonald's long assembly has made all the ink writing run together with the sweat, and you can't make anything out. I tell him he'll need a palm reader with him in the exam. He'll have to go into the English exam with only his wooden ruler. He holds it very carefully, like it's radioactive, for fear of smudging. The Bike has concertinaed wads of paper in his mouth with passages of Shakespeare and other works. He'll pull them out like an accordion along the length of his arm on the desk.

No one regards any of this as cheating. Life is not a memory test but the exams are. How can you test a person's ability for a year's work with one three-hour test? What if you have a brain explosion during the exam, as you tend to do when you see the questions you prepared aren't anywhere in the paper? If you can't trust the teachers, who can you trust?

For as long as I can remember, I've always brought

the same writing materials into an exam. A Bic clear
biro, which has recently been allowed by a Papal Bull
out of the Vatican to be used by Catholics instead of
fountain pens. A spare biro in case the first one runs
out of ink or gets stuck because I poke it in my ear-
hole, as you do, when it itches. Georgina once asked
me if I had a tattoo in my ear but I eventually worked
out it was just ink from the Bic. If you dismantle a
Bic, the clear casing makes a great peashooter and the
skinny cartridge can reach right through to the eardrum.
My lucky elephant rubber has been worn as smooth
as a river stone by mistakes. A wooden varnished ruler
from Blakes Busy Book Bazaar with inches and cen-
timetres marked on either side. There's no writing
because of the varnish but it's my lucky ruler so I can't
change it. Everything is kept together in a bundled roll
with a couple of twists of a thick rubber band.

All the repeaters walk down Salisbury Road to the
Great Hall at St Charles in silence, although everyone's
lips are moving. St Charles is a primary school, so when
we enter the not-so-great hall we see that all the desks
and chairs were made for primary kids. You can barely
get one cheek of your arse onto the chair and you have
to clutch hard to stay steady. We're giants in a school
for pygmies. It's a bit undermining to be sitting for
Leaving Certificate English in a room whose walls are
covered with drawings of stick figures on cardboard
done by the kindergarten, cloth quilted alphabets with
black letters and objects like an apple in the A box

hanging from the ceiling and The cat sat on the mat written in chalk on the blackboard. No wonder kindergarten is a breeze. All the answers are right in front of you. Simmo checks under his seat to see if there's a potty. It does prick your balloon somewhat.

The small desktops make writing hard, and I have to use my lucky rubber a lot. We're seated in alphabetical order. From the back row I can see Simmo, Grantie, The Bike and all the others lifting the cuffs of their trousers, trying to read the notes on their legs, rolling up their sleeves, revealing themselves like tattooed persons at the Show, pulling papers out of their mouths in long wet streamers and reading them like tickertape. Simmo initially panics as he can't make out his own handwriting on his ruler, but settles down as he turns it into the sunlight from the side window.

The examiners walk up and down between the little desks as we hunch over the papers, hiding everything from their X-ray vision. English is divided into two sections, literature and language. English language has gone to the dogs. One assignment is to write 600 words about a photo in the exam paper. Heaven knows what that has to do with English language. Mein Furner hasn't prepared us for this sort of exercise. It doesn't matter how many lines you know out of *The Rime of the Ancient Mariner*, they won't help you write 600 words about a photo of a tiger jumping through a hoop in the centre ring of a packed circus tent. They've caught the Unchristian Brothers with their pants down.

One of the advantages of a top-notch Unchristian Brothers education is the access to the pooled resources of years of solid teaching and the copies of each year's Leaving Certificate exams going back to the invention of the printing press and beyond. But never before has there been a question like this. Never has there been a photo in an English exam. Tut tut tut is all Moffitt himself can say later when he sees the question. He recovers and says it's the end of education as we know it. Writing's got nothing to do with English. How can boys be expected to prepare for an exam if they can't learn off by heart the answers to the questions? It's not natural to expect a boy just to make something up on the spot like that. We all curse the Wyndham Scheme and its Protestants.

The tiger picture presents a problem that couldn't be solved even if you'd written all over your body and had a mouthful of notes. The obvious thing to do is to write about the tiger from the tiger's point of view. Like, I'm sick of running around in circles kind of thing. I pick out a face from the crowd and write about his life. The story has nothing to do with the tiger, the tiger tamer or the circus. The guy had found a ticket on the street where he slept. He was a down and out and nothing good had ever happened to him. He had no job, no family and lived in a cardboard box under the railway station. Just as he was about to jump into the path of a steam engine he looked down at his feet and saw a bright ticket, which turned out to be to this very circus for that very day. Instead of jumping to his death that morning, he went to the circus and saw the tigers. They lived in cages like him. I won't bore you further with the details because 600 words is a lot, even counting very small ones like the and and. He left the circus performance and jumped under the evening train.

The worst words a guy can ever hear during the last weeks of school are Ten minutes, Ten minutes to go. The whole room lets out a collective *What?* and checks their watches—carefully, without showing any forearm. You can't hear the traffic on Salisbury Road for the scratching of pens in that last ten minutes. The day-light saving has robbed us of an hour and the last ten minutes gallop like Tulloch until those crushing final words: Pens down. Just a few more words ... Pens down.

The Unchristian Brothers have taught us that more is more. The more words the better. In fact the Brothers mark their exams on the weight of the homework. Simmo always uses plenty of staples to keep the top corners together. He believes it gives his work heft. But the public examiners don't do a word count when marking. That's why they set a 600 word limit. It's a plot to defeat the lines theory of education. Under the Brothers, if you run out of words to say in an exam on say The Great Depression you just keep writing and maybe repeating everything you wrote earlier. In front of the class Moffitt's eyes lift appreciatively if he sees six, seven or, eyes popping, eight pages. With Simmo, he holds it in one hand and lifts it up and down a little, saying Great work. The paper looks like an Indian nail-bed on its underside.

When I die I know that all I'll hear will be God booming over a loudspeaker in the sky: Pens down. Waterstreet, didn't you hear me boy? Pens down. Perhaps he'll flick a finger of chalk at me. Pens down. Life goes from a slap on the arse to Pens down before you know it.

After the allegedly three hours but more like three minutes, we walk back up Salisbury Road in stunned despair, dropping notes and pieces of paper out of our pockets and socks like Hansel and Gretel. Simmo sums up the situation, as usual: What a bummer. The paper should have been headed '19666 English Examination'. He licks his forearms clean of ink using plenty of spit like a cat.

Not even the sight of Georgina and Katie walking towards us from Theo's Hot Chips and Sandwiches can cheer me up. Grantie says photography isn't a subject, so why the fuck did they put one in the exam, an English exam for Christ's sake. We walk under the proud wrought iron Latin school motto with our hearts in our hands. School shields with Latin mottos should have subtitles for those without language skills. Otherwise they might think it was just bad spelling.

Tomorrow is Modern History. We feel that we were fucking history today. I remember when Mein Furner asked the class for the causes of World War I and Simmo threw his hand into the air and waved it up and down so enthusiastically you'd think he was pulling the chain. Yes sonny. He calls everyone sonny. Well, sir, fighting. It was the fighting. Even Furner couldn't argue with that, but of course being the bastard he was he did. Then Furner threw Simmo out of the class for a perfectly accurate answer. Teachers today. You gotta question them.

That sort of education hasn't prepared us for questions about photographs of tigers. As examinees we could have used a few more cheerleaders like Georgina and Katie, perhaps the junior school running up and down outside the Great Hall with a couple of Double Waverleys. School is so hung up on sport. It doesn't really care for the other parts of a guy's life, like education. The school's Honour Board for football and cricket is in gold lettering with finely turned cedar panelling. The Dux of College board is in plain black paint. Dad is throwing away his hard-earned SP bookie and Sunday trading money on these fees. I feel like I've been running on the spot for the whole year.

There's barely time for most of the boys to rub the writing off their rulers and to write out a year's worth of Modern History for tomorrow. I've dropped Latin for Modern History this year because it is slowly dawning on me that very few people outside the school grounds are speaking Latin and in fact no one had actually used the language for over a thousand years.

You aren't likely to meet a chick at the beach from overseas and start chatting her up in Latin. Latin lovers is I'm afraid an ironic phrase.

Whereas I'm fascinated by the pictures in the World War II books. In the school library, high up on the top shelf, above the colouring-in books, I gaze at the black and white photo books of concentration camps and hundreds of dead Jewish people lying naked on each other in gigantic tomb pits. On the ladder in the library is as close to a dead body as I've come. The pictures transfix me. Tractors as pallbearers. Modern History, I think, will explain why. There is more than a tinge of the erotic or something that lived next door to it in the nude women's bodies. I try not to dwell on it for fear of being thought of as a necrophiliac, but then nobody can read my thoughts. But can they? The whole process of standing on the ladder staring at the photos and thinking these thoughts makes me giddy and guilty at the same time. Even the facade of studying Modern History doesn't help explain it, so I stick to the text as best I can. Dad's barber shop magazines under his bed don't have full nudes, just boobs and bums. No bush. Yet Waverley College's library has full frontals right under the Brothers' noses. I cackle and keep it to myself.

At nine sharp the next morning it's Pens up followed by the furious movements of pens, biros and pencils on paper and correcting the spellings of Mussolini and Weimar and the impossible Treaty of Versailles. At least there are no photos, except the compelling ones in my mind's eye from the top shelf. Modern History is a lot easier than Ancient History because there are photos and films of it to look at and check out. There's footage to confirm it. Photography hadn't been invented in Ancient History and drawings of fighting centurions in tunics bore the shit out of me. The Greeks look like cartoons.

It's Pens up and Pens down for two weeks. Brother McMahon gives last-minute instructions in Mathematics. Don't put a stroke in number seven. It's a dead giveaway of a Catholic education and they'll mark you down because of it. We hope that the constant scribbling out of sevens and their corrections in the exam go unnoticed by the Protestant markers of the Department of Education. Catholics are the Jews of Australia.

Most of the guys have written all over their hands for Physics and Chemistry. The elements and compounds and the mighty atom's molecular structure are not things you ordinarily carry in your head, but somehow I have a knack for them so my hands are clear for these subjects. Milliken's Oil Can Experiment is something I know backwards. I love formulas or formulae as Brother McMahon put it, but don't dare write that in the Chemistry exam. They'll pick you up as a Catholic quick smart. Simmo says that it would be hard to disguise being a Catholic in the Latin exam but McMahon waves him off with a backward gesture as if he were swatting a handball away. The book in the library shows me that the Germans are cruel and hard markers.

Theo's Hot Chips and Sandwiches nearly goes broke during the exams because we are all too frightened and scared shitless to eat. We live on the plastic at the top of our biros. Even Georgina and Katie go off their tucker during this time, in sympathy with us. You shouldn't have to do exams when you're in love because it's hard to do your best when your mind's somewhere else. They say the left-hand side of your brain does the creative stuff and the right-hand side does the Maths and laundry. During the exams both sides are fighting with each other to keep Georgina out of the picture and Maths and Physics in the frame. It's well nigh impossible, and before the last exam in Chemistry I can't wait any longer and meet her on the slope behind the goalpost in Queens Park.

I tell her, not that I believe in it, but the whole exam process is anti-Catholic. How do you know? There's no exam in Religious Knowledge. That's lucky for you, she laughs. Our lips collide and passers-by can probably hear the clink of our teeth against each other's as if cheering each other with porcelain cups. There's sure to be a yellow patch of our outline on the grass from the heat when we get up. My whole body's got lover's balls. I think I'll die of it. I'll be buried on the slopes of Queens Park. My tombstone will read Died of lover's balls. Pens down in 1966. Mourners will tut tut It's the way he'd have wanted to go. With his sandshoes on.

There's been talk of a phenomenon known as the dry root. According to Grantie, when you're kissing and hugging you lie on top of the girl and hump her in your clothes and she in hers like you're fucking, but fully clothed, and you come in your underpants. Before you know it I'm dry-rooting Georgina fully clothed with my sandshoe tips digging deeply into the turf lest we roll down the hill and onto the freshly cut pitch. It actually hurts a bit. Dry-rooting should be done without a brass zipper or Y-fronts, but it isn't long at all before I come, groaning at the top of my voice Georgina, Georgina. Her name is quite a mouthful but there's no way to shorten it. In the old days you had to call out their surname as well.

How long has this dry-rooting been going on I'd like to know. My God it feels good, despite the zipper. It's a pity Georgina can't join me. I've heard a rumour at school that girls come too, but it seems like an urban myth. They don't have cocks or balls. There's a bit of bullshit out there about sex, and you have to know how to sort the wheat from the chaff if you want to get some. Next thing they'll be saying that girls enjoy sex as much as us.

The dry root lifts my spirits enormously when I tell everyone about it when I get back. Finally, I think, I can concentrate on Chemistry. But the funny thing is I keep on thinking about it more than ever. I want another dry root more than anything. Even after I nearly pass out peeling my underpants off.

* * *

Mein Furner loves his glass prism. Every year in Physics he takes it into the final year class and shows its magical qualities. So he's mightily pissed off when Simmo borrows it to show the girls at Theo's Hot Chips and Sandwiches. The exams are over and we're just killing time until we're allowed to go home. It's the size of a football, with equal sides. The edges are as sharp as razor blades. When you hold it in your hands it feels nice and heavy and makes you feel like a million pounds, which this year would be two million dollars since February 14th.

Furner treats it like a tabernacle, keeping it on top of his bedside table in his room. When you hold it up to the light you can see all the colours of the spectrum on the other side of the room. Simmo has Theo and the girls in the palm of his hand as he slowly turns the prism while the colours of the rainbow turn on the greasy white walls. Simmo has taken it because Katie has heard about the prism from Georgina, who heard about it from me. When Simmo drops it because of the oil from the chips on his hands onto Theo's floor it shatters into thousands of pieces across the lino. Mein Furner's heart must have shattered at the same time, but if he sensed it he doesn't fully realise it until Simmo and I hand him the green garbage bag Theo gave us, full of most of the thousands of pieces of his prize prism. We thought he'd be a lot more angry. He looks like he's lost his best friend. He just takes it back into his room, locking the door behind him.

The Last Leaving

The last few days at Waverley College are like living on a dude ranch. The rest of the school have their own exams and it's prayers on knees just out of bed, Mass in the Chapel, grace before meals, grace after meals, morning prayer, midday Angelus, prayers before each subject, prayers after each subject, prayers before lunch, prayers after lunch, the Litany at three o'clock in the afternoon, prayers at the end of class, prayers and rosary before dinner, grace before and after dinner, prayers before homework, prayers after homework, and finally prayers before bed. Then straight to bed for hand to hand conflict with the Devil himself, enriched by the squeezing of a window frame on the forearm.

But we repeating boarders can come and go as we please. Simmo wants to sublet his bed and make a profit. The Bike stays on a few days even though he lives a stone's throw away, even with my arm. In fact it's his parents who insist he stay on, until their fees are well and truly exhausted. He says that they paid for a full term and weren't going to be gypped of a few days by the Brothers. Men's and women's plumbing doctors work on time and not emotion.

We are allowed to sleep in, not go to Mass and skip meals if we want. We wear day clothes and act like lords of the manor. Many Brothers envy us, especially Moffitt who's keen to try an upper cut at close range. Simmo's red transistor plays at full blare in the dorm while we lie in bed reading the *Daily Telegraph*, looking for a movie to see, maybe later in the day.

After the initial no more teachers, no more books, no more teacher's crazy looks feeling has faded, we all suffer a touch of the blues. The new fifth formers, the first class of Wyndham Education Schemers, are the new breed. Old Macdonald describes them as guinea pigs preparing for a press-button society. They are goods whose delivery has been postponed a year to give extra finish. We feel like dinosaurs at sixteen. They are pioneers. We are a period piece. Then there is the long wait for our results and summer jobs for some and back onto the Massey Ferguson tractor for others. The best years are behind us or out of reach. We are in no man's land.

When bitten by the black dog like this Simmo brings a smile to our faces with his stories. He remembers the time I was an altar boy at Benediction for Father Keneally from the church at Charing Cross. It was my last time. I wasn't asked back after that. Benediction is big business. It's a short Mass held on Sunday evening at about dusk. It's all pomp and transubstantiation. Simmo says At the risk of making a story too long. No risk pipes The Bike. When you're in third year one of the boarders' jobs in rotation is to pick up the communion hosts from the Carmelite nuns who live in strict seclusion next to the Mary Immaculate Church at Charing Cross. Two boarders. And by complete serendipity Simmo and I found ourselves walking down Salisbury Street and then into Campbell Street after school with an empty Arnotts biscuit tin.

Next to the Mary Immaculate was a Presbytery for Father Keneally and his jolly band of Friar Tucks in brown robes with hoods and white ropes around their tummies. They were Franciscans. Part of the Presbytery was the hangout for the Carmelite nuns. It was completely closed off to the rest of the world, including if you don't mind Father Keneally himself. Carmelites take the vow of silence which is really hard for the Irish. They also vow never to look at another human being or be looked at. Simmo believed they must have been real ugly. All the doors and windows of their part of the Presbytery were painted over. You could neither look in nor look out. They never left, and only Father Keneally came in and then he said Mass behind a screen so he couldn't see them nor they him.

We rang the bell at the front door and walked into a highly varnished foyer with a cross here and there on the walls. The Carmelites' job was to make and bake big hosts of communion for Benediction and the priest and little hosts for the riff raff. The biscuit tin was for carrying these hosts back to school for the chapel pantry. Set into one wall was a curved cedar-wood lazy susan with half wood panelling. When the nuns turned the lazy susan halfway there was always a boarded barrier between them and the other side. I put the biscuit tin on the lazy susan and the nun I presumed turned the wooden panelling halfway round to get it without perving. However, at each side of the panelling there was a crack. Simmo had his eye opened and hard against one crack as did I on the other. These women hadn't seen a male for up to forty or fifty years, or another female for that matter, except each other. No one had seen them. We thought they might die with our gaze. Or we might be struck dead or blinded. In fact they giggled like girls as our single ogling eyes stuck through the cracks like periscopes. They certainly needed a bit of time on a towel down at Bronte Beach. They were as pale as hen's eggs, heads covered in brown habits. But even the oldest looked like a teenager. They looked up and down and tittered while filling the biscuit tin to overflowing with hosts. The panelling turned and we rushed out lest our luck changed.

We walked back to school feasting on the big and smaller hosts to our sacred heart's content. The body of Our Lord and Saviour before he assumes human form in the shape of a communion host is mighty tasty. He is a bit like Jatz crackers. Once you have one you want another. Jesus is very more-ish. By the time we got back to school we had devoured half of Our Lord and Saviour in small size and there were none in large. We were really peckish. We put the tin in the sanctuary and later told Father Keneally that the nuns only gave us half a tin. The Carmelites were shorting the Brothers on the body of Jesus Christ.

That's nothing compared to when Charlie took off with Jesus Christ himself, adds Simmo. Another task of third year boarders was to serve as altar boys at Mass and Benediction. Although I had been to thousands of Benedictions I hadn't taken all that much notice of the order of things. I loved the songs and the smell of incense and the ceremony had more pizzazz than Mass. But the choreography had me beat. At one stage the altar boy is supposed to get the wine and water from the side and take it to the priest. At another stage the priest gets the monstrance from the high altar. The monstrance is a goldburst sun on a solid gold stand. It has a glass window in the middle where the sacred host is placed and it has clear glass so, unlike Carmelites, we can see him in host form and he can see us and the priest holds the monstrance up and shows it around the church as if it were the Bledisloe Cup won in a tight game. The point is that no one whose hands haven't been blessed with Holy Orders can hold Jesus Christ. The nuns can and the biscuit tin holders could because he hadn't been transubstantiated yet, that is the host hadn't been turned into Jesus by the magic words. Catholics believe that once the priest says Abracadabra the host is really, I'm not kidding, really the body of the big feller and the wine is no longer Seppelt's sherry sweet or dry but his blood. Old priests drink it down like vampires. In glorious excess his blood still makes a priest tipsy.

One time Charlie wandered off during Benediction, says Simmo. The incense drugged me, I pipe in. I take up the running of the gag while we gather around Simmo's bed because he has the only trannie. I was just daydreaming and a bell went off in my ear, rung by the other altar server. I'd lost the plot and thought that I should do something. I jumped to my feet. The priest was at the lower altar fiddling about. I walked smartly to the side and up the marble stairs behind the front altar. As I mounted them I did hear a sudden inward gasp for air from the two hundred or so boys and Brothers to my side. I wondered what was going on, but I was intent on sticking to my job which I thought was to grab the golden monstrance by the stem, which I did, and turn around and walk with it slowly down the stairs and place it in the middle of the altar.

All the air previously held in the congregation's lungs came out in one gigantic exhalation. I felt I was in a wind tunnel so I held the monstrance even tighter lest I drop it. Father Keneally threw his sacred white hands in the air and rushed at me. I thought he was going to tackle me. I lost the track completely. Was I at Bene-diction or footy practice? He ripped the monstrance off me after a tug of war and rushed it to the altar like it was a just-delivered baby. There there. I stared at the two hundred faces in chapel and they stared back, mouths gaping as if for little communion hosts. Brothers crossed themselves as it witnessing a kick for goal at Queens Park.

Apparently I was supposed to get the water and wine and the priest gets the monstrance. In fact at that stage the monstrance actually had the consecrated big host, the family sized one, in the round glass window. No one but priests with ordained and bishop-blessed hands were allowed to even touch the monstrance. It was a sacred site on a sacred stand in a sacred place. Frankly he didn't seem that heavy and, being one of the very few unblessed people who have actually carried him for a bit, I felt kind of special. But that wasn't the way the priest or Brothers saw it. I was sidelined for life as an altar boy. It was regarded as worse than punching the ref out. I was in the sin bin forever.

We keep up story after story until our stomachs ache for food. The rest of the school is in class but we few, we lucky few, are still in shortie pyjamas listening to the Dave Clark Five and static. Mein Furner goosesteps into the dorm and looks at us very crossly. Most of the repeaters have left, either to Mass like goody-two-shoes Roger Ng, or to a late breakfast. His sudden appearance ungathers our robust get-together and we saunter into the locker room slightly crushed and ill at ease. After all, we're men of the world now, our schooldays behind us, and to be clapped into silence by the Furner is a kick in the shins. We are men of rope not string.

* * *

One of the day boys in the repeating year organises a huge party for Saturday night. No parents. There's to be a keg of beer and all the frankfurters you can eat, wrapped in white bread with tomato sauce. Simmo and I book a hotel room for ourselves at the Carlton Rex at Kings Cross. I reckon I might be in with a chance with Georgina, and Simmo has his eye on Katie. We're prepared to pay for free love.

Our pockets are full of loose change which jangles in our jeans as we walk down Birrell Street like Aly Khans before turning right on Alfred, left on Howlett and down to Miramar Street where the McGilloolys have left their eldest son and repeater Bill in charge for the weekend. The McGillooly backyard looks over Tamarama bay and beach. It's rumoured girls sunbathe on Tamarama on their stomachs with their bra straps undone. The McGilloolys' house must be worth a fortune if that's true because with a telescope you could just about reach out and touch the rocks on the Bondi side of the beach. The back fence, over the years, has taken a tremendous pounding from the salt, wind, cricket balls and curiosity seekers, and the planks are practically floorboards rather than pickets. The back lawn is bleached yellow around the back cement steps, where generations of McGillooly men have relieved themselves. Never into the relentless wind that blows from the sea, but to the side, where it falls onto the lawn or in a fair storm under the house. The Hills hoist grows like a steel toadstool plum in the middle. The garage on the side of the house is purpose-built for a nine-gallon keg, barbecue fire and an old tin bath with ice for the bottles, and Mr McGillooly's shelving for his tools is perfectly placed to hold a stereo with giant 12-inch twin speakers.

The Bike has taken up residence again at home. He brings a stack of his parents' records, which we use for plates because the sauce drips everywhere if you're not careful. The family stereo has all three speeds but the only way their LPs are any use at the McGilloolys is as plates or frisbees. The shy boys read the album covers to themselves under the swinging Osram light bulb while McGillooly's little sisters stack piles of ten 45s together in groups of slow, medium and fast music. There's a pile of albums for later in the evening, when the young McGilloolys will have dropped off to sleep. Bill has everything in place except his parents' permission. There are rolls of toilet paper for the ladies' fingers and careless crumbs, and a bottle of soft drink for anyone who dares.

It's way past nine before the girls arrive spic and span. Georgina brings a biscuit tin of baklava her mother baked this afternoon. Her Scottish mother has, like many converts, taken to late onset adult Greek descent with more vigour than those born to it. She has dolmades for breakfast, calamari for lunch and goat for dinner. I wouldn't be surprised if she grew a moustache and a widow's hump.

Bill has borrowed a T-piece Extractor and Pluto beer gun from the Robin Hood pub. I have to tap the keg and end up covered in froth and stinking of beer. I run my hands through my hair to dry them. The man who taps a keg has to know what he's on about. It's not a skill that Georgina admires as much as I'd like. She's more into retsina and raisins. But in any language she's a fox, a feisty fiery fox. But barmen are not high on the list of people Greek daughters want to make love to, marry and settle down with for life. That much I can see under her bangs and in her eyes. I feel it when I'm filling Mrs McGillooly's china teacups with beer for the queue of thirsty teenagers. I'm supposed to leave my luggage behind and accommodate hers, which is more than enough for two. I would willingly drop my entire heritage, my Mum and Dad, my aunts and uncles, my hitherto so-called life for her. I'll learn Greek, give Greek, take Greek, become Greek. I want her. I want her to myself.

Simmo is playing the Latin lover to Katie. He actually speaks in Latin, and Latin only. He sticks his tongue out and wiggles it, slurring out I speak in many tongues. He looks like a dirty drover's dog with an erection. Katie is enthralled. She's putty in his hands.

Soon we're all doing the Stomp in the McGilloolys' garage off and on as the needle jumps on the stereo from the vibrations through the cement floor. You don't need cardboard cut-out feet like Arthur Murray's to be able to Stomp. You just need feet. One up, the other down. Other up, other down. It takes me a little time to master, with my two left feet, but after a couple of cups of beer without a saucer I'm Mr Rhythm and Georgina is twisting up and down an imaginary fire-pole.

The slow music and dancing come to me like magic. I just lean over Georgina and turn slowly in a circle with other couples. You just make it up on the spot. Like the hitchhiker, pulling the toilet chain and the runaway semaphore. I bury my face at right angles to my neck in Georgina's jet-black hair, my hands on her hips, then bum, her hands on mine and back to the hips. She talks to me about the Vietnam War through the slow stuff like Spicks and Specks. I agree with everything she says, even when I can't hear.

Love means having no other greasy-palmed youth pawing over your girlfriend. All I can see in my mind's eye, playing continuously in wide screen technicolor 3-D, is Cranky O'Brien's bitten fingernails and broken fingers from the bottom of collapsed scrums cupped over Georgina's breasts. It drives me mad. Cranky taps me on the shoulder to break in during Eleanor Rigby. He earned his nickname before he drained Mr McGillooly's bottom drawer of Jameson's Irish whisky.

I now yearn for just plain old Cranky. He is supersonic pissed off, steaming and frothing at the mouth. I have little alternative, with the yellow streak painted from the back of my neck down to the heels of my feet, but to hand Georgina over. A lesser man might have made a scene. But I turn on the spot and search for Simmo and the boys. After all, it's our last night together as schoolmates. After tonight we'll just be mates.

Simmo is sinking frankfurters in and out of Katie's mouth. Georgina'll handle it, he says. I feel myself going green with yellow stripe. I don't want to look around at them but my eyes have a mind of their own and catch the one-time lovers in mid-spin. Georgina is twirling under Cranky's outstretched hand. My stomach churns. Love is the pits. Simmo puts his arm around me and draws me in close. I can smell his Brylcreem at the tip of my nose. Don't show it. Act like you couldn't care less. You'll have her eating out of your hand before midnight. I look at my watch. I'll have to work fast. It's eleven thirty.

When a group of Waverlians get together, not much time passes before you're singing Faith of Our Fathers, Holy Queen of Heaven and shouting the Double Waverley. We're now imbued with the mighty juice of the gods, beer, and as Simmo predicted Georgina joins me with a hug and Cranky storms out of the garage door to take it out on the garbage bins standing defiantly in his way down Miramar Street. The neighbours call the police, who come straight through the garage door without so much as a beg your pardon and turn the volume knob down to nought. The police are the Brothers of our new world. Pigs! shouts Georgina, still angry over Johnson's visit. The sergeant mimics a backhander but backs off. But it's the kiss of death to the party. I'll see you soon. Bye. Ta ta. Thanks for a great night. Need any help? Catch you later. Fan-fucking-tastic. Same time. Same place. Every night. Thanks for coming.

It's all over. See you.

Georgina goes home early after I throw up the second time on the way to Theo's Hot Chips and Sandwiches.

The Rex has about twenty floors of rooms and Simmo and I have a lot of fun switching the shoes that were left outside each room for cleaning to other rooms on other floors. It's a pity we aren't awake in time to see the patrons' reactions when they wake in the morning to find stilettos instead of brogues. The lobby is full of people walking on tippy-toes in socks holding shoes at arm's length, looking for their rightful partners.

***

I pack up my luggage at school. I shake hands with everyone, including Moffitt, who squeezes really hard. I'm not going to miss school at all, but I'm sure going to miss Simmo and the boys. We promise to keep in touch.

171

I ring Georgina from the pay phone at Central. She says she'll come for a week before Christmas. Great. My stomach turns. It isn't something I ate. Can't wait. Me too. Me too.

The train conductor is old Curly McPherson who fixes me up with a cabin of my own where I can stretch out to sleep. I take off my school uniform for the last time in the toilet in car three of the Spirit of Progress just as it pulls out of Strathfield. I sleep until Goulburn, where there are pies and peas for sale in the middle of the night. I read *Henry V* for the first time straight through. It probably would have been better to do it before the exams. It's a pretty ripping yarn.

Once the Spirit of Progress hits Henty it's practically downhill all the way to Albury. You could swear that Mrs Westie's burnt bacon and eggs are smellable by the time we stop at Culcairn international railway station, gateway to Walla Walla and Mungabareena. By Gerogery I have all my bags poised next to the door near the rubberised accordion walkway connecting my carriage to the next one. Curly unlocks the door for me. He knows of Westie's cooking. The Spirit is not supposed to stop again before Albury but some toff from Table Top must have pulled his weight and the train pulls to a jerky stop for the sleeping berth carriage to pull alongside the short platform so he can get off and return to his herd of Best of Show 1966 Murray Greys grazing on his endless farm.

Normally Mrs Westie's cooking is not your mouthwatering dream, but this time, after months of boarding school beans and bangers, the time at Table Top doesn't seem to be postponing the inedible. When Curly's voice announces Next stop Albury Railway Station I open the door and feel the breeze rushing into the carriage, chilling my face and blowing my hair back like a wind tunnel. Over the tops of one-storey skyscrapers I see the white stick-like War Memorial where Dad told me all Albury's war dead were buried. The things parents tell you as a kid—and they wonder why we want to form our own generation. A litany of lies from Santa Claus to the Easter Bunny to Jesus Christ through to Vietnam and now no sex before marriage. Ha.

I throw my bags out near the entrance while the train is still moving so as to save trudging half the length of the fourth or fifth longest platform in the southern hemisphere. The bags tumble over until one bursts open, throwing out my striped pyjamas, socks, singlets and underpants with skidmarks for the rest of the passengers to see. Curly helps me pick them up quickly, noting over his breath that my Y-fronts seem a bit tobacco-stained. Yeah. Thanks.

Five years of boarding school are packed into four bags, including Colin Simpson's *The Big Country* prize for Dux. The book itself is as heavy as a butcher's block. So I borrow a porter's trolley with four wheels and ride it down Smollett Street like a billycart until I'm under the verandah of Waterstreets Hotel.

Hotel Sweet Hotel

Of course we're close, I know all my immediate family on a first-name basis, but I don't know whether or not Mum is home or in hospital or wherever. I mount the stairs expecting the unexpected and ready for it. Dad is eating breakfast in bed, reading the *Border Morning Mail* back to front through the cigarette haze, and there is no dent in the pillows on Mum's side so I guess she isn't there. I show him my prizes and go downstairs to the hotel kitchen.

Katherine Ann is in boarding school a hundred yards down the road, and Peter, John and Paul Damien (aka The Hood) are eating rice bubbles that stick to their lips like warts. I pretend I know where Mum is and wait for information about her to overhear. A guy can't just ask. That would imply that no one has bothered to tell him, and that would reflect badly all round.

Bit by bit I put together that she is back in Kenmore Hospital. Last night she'd been a stone's throw from me when I gobbled down my pie and peas at Goulburn railway station in the early morning cold to feed my own mild horsepower. In my cold heart I would rather she wasn't here at home if she wasn't herself. In the last few years it's been hard to distinguish her from those poor souls downstairs. Her life has gone from bad to worse. When she's at home in bed under the kangaroo-skin cover we walk through the hallway quietly on the pads of our feet as if on broken glass. In her absence we gallop down the hall and bound onto the stairs, but inside it is unbearable and unspoken.

The boys are waiting for Mrs Westie to finish placing the big cold chunks of meat onto margarine-smeared slabs of warm baked bread. Then she pats the bottom of the IXL tomato sauce bottle like a baby three times and positions another white warm slab of bread on top and presses down on them with the side of a meat chopper until the sauce squits out as if shot, and she wraps them in used oilpaper with neat hospital corners giving Peter, John and The Hood their playlunch which they'll swap for lollies at school.

Their ears prick up when I enquire of Mrs Westie whether she can cook anything Greek as I have a friend, wink wink, coming from Sydney to stay. Her name is Georgina George, if you must know. Now piss off or you'll miss the bus. The Hood says he doesn't go on the bus. He's still at St Patrick's. A Hume Weir sized wave of nostalgia sweeps over me when I shoo them off in their summer shorts and green and gold ties. I will never again wear the green and gold or the blue and gold. I comfort myself with the thought that I'll wear only paisley from this point on. It suits my complexion.

Mrs Westie consults her miracle cookbook that's wedged under the meat locker. She's written down with a blunt pencil through the years in an old schoolbook with lined pages all the wonders and secrets of her cuisine. It has so much gravy and gunk on it you could feed a small army a page at a time for months. She mutters Greek, Greek, Greek as she thumbs each page, licking it every time with a smack of her lips as if taking delight in delicious cook-ups past. Greek Greek Greek. Leave it to me, Charlie, she'll feel as if she never left home. We'll eat out a lot I think to myself, which is really the best person to think to when you come to think about it.

Upstairs in two mighty leaps I see Dad has dozed off but has the newspaper tucked under his belly. I pull it out, one crumpled but ever so quiet page at a time. It smells of burnt toast. His lips quiver like the sides of a hovercraft but he doesn't wake.

Lady Luck is smiling on me. I've landed in Albury in the middle of the judging of the Zhivago-look quest. Girls between sixteen and twenty face the judges at Mates Ltd showrooms during a parade starting at 12.45 p.m. sharp. Every chick in the Greater Albury District has entered or has been entered by an enthusiastic parent. The movie is so popular it has a morning, afternoon and night session at the Regent. The *Border* reviewer said *Doctor Zhivago* made up for all the bad films that had gone before it. He said it was better than the translation of the book, but he was critical of the flashbacks presentation, clever as it was. Albury is in the grip of Zhivago fever.

My old friend Taillight is working at the railway so he has nothing to do, so we walk down to Mates to see the contestants vying for the final cash prize of $100 for the girl judged most like the star of the film. Mates is chock-a-block with girls from as far away as Burrumbuttock, all in white headscarves wrapped tightly around their necks and the tops of their heads. Only black and blonde bangs of hair over the forehead show. It doesn't matter what else the contestants wear. It's the head that counts. So hundreds of Julie Christie unlookalikes walk up and down the women's wear section of Mates on the second floor, hoping to catch the judges' eyes. Some wear dresses, some jeans, some overalls. But otherwise their winter-grim faces glare from the wrapped scarves and under the bangs towards the four judges making notes on their clipboards. A man in a fur hat could do well here, says Taillight. He's seen the film to kill time while he's working. It's a bit on the mushy side for him. *The Liquidator* with Rod Taylor is coming to Hoyts and he'll whiz down there from work when it opens. He left school after the Intermediate Certificate by mutual agreement and joined the New South Wales Government Railways before deciding what he wants to do in life.

It's a funny thing, but when people get into costume they take on the character. All the Julie Christies look like they're at a funeral, grim-faced, haunted, lost and in the midst of impossible love. We can't crack a smile out of any of the stony-faced Julies. They look like a tribe of lost nuns emerging from the jungle in prayer. I think it might suddenly snow in Mates in November.

Taillight tells me he scored a chick long ago and didn't have to pay much at all. He's way ahead in the life department. When I tell him that Georgina is coming and would have won the Zhivago-look quest by a furlong he gives me That Look from beneath his albino eyelashes. No, I haven't yet but it's only a matter of time, I assure him.

The final contestants are named over Mates's loud-speaker system and many Julie Christies burst into real tears when their names aren't mentioned. Some snatch their veils off their heads and march off in huffs. The winners keep their scarves on and walk down Dean Street peering into the distance for Dr Zhivago to arrive by train from Moscow via Wagga Wagga. There are short Julie Christies, fat and skinny Julie Christies, blonde, black and brown Julie Christies, pimply, freck-led and lipsticked Julie Christies. Dean Street chokes with slow-walking Julie Christies, oblivious to Taillight and me who by now have wrapped handkerchiefs over our heads in sympathy. We're one of them, if only they could see it. Zhivago, Zhivago; it's not my kind of town.

* * *

Dad insists I get a job for the summer while we wait for the exam results, even though the results are really only of academic interest. I'm beginning to doubt my vocation because I have no idea what doctors do. I don't know any, except Marcus Welby MD. I put down medicine in the Commonwealth Scholarship application last year because I have some sort of knack in Physics and Chemistry, and that's the closest option. I can't repeat the leaving again so life, real life, is staring me in the face and I can't bear to look back. Perhaps Mum's lack of success with doctors dampens what little enthusiasm I can muster.

Dad arranges with the Station Master that a new position be organised at the railway to accommodate me for the school holidays. I'm the first and last junior temporary permanent station attendant in the long and magnificent history of New South Wales Government Railways. (NSWGR on tea towels and government toilet paper regularly and mysteriously appeared as part of our hotel's facilities and sanitary services.) The Station Master tells me to bring two books with me for the first day. Why? You'll get through more than one. It sounds like it's just the job for a guy with time on his hands and a week before his first girlfriend comes by rail from Sydney.

I've been seriously misled, Dad, I tell him after my first day. He smiles and puts the terry towel bar napkin over his right shoulder and asks why. The men at the bar are listening in with their huge old men's ears. The job has two parts. One part is weighing the freight of trains that leave Albury station. That part isn't too hard. At the back of the railway yards is a huge revolving weigh station where each loaded carriage is weighed before being shunted onto the train. A shunter writes the results on a card and places it in a metal holder on the side of the train. I write down the complete weight on each card and take away the empty weight of each carriage. Voila, the weight of the freight. It isn't complicated but you need all your fingers to do the maths.

The second part of the job has to do with passenger trains. This is the part where I feel the years of schooling have been wasted. James Watt might have been a genius when he invented the steam engine but it was a pity he didn't spend some time on the carriage. When a train goes from Albury to another metropolis like Sydney, the likelihood is that a person will have to go at least once to the toilet. Now the odds on that have been multiplied with the straight-through gauge joining Melbourne to Sydney. Each carriage has a toilet with a bowl that goes straight down in a hole. If a person has a crap while the train is steaming between Benalla and Beechworth it's not a worry, except to that person who might feel the wind up them. People who live between Benalla and Beechworth don't mind because the track is out in the middle of Woop Woop and it keeps the flies away from their places. However, when the train is at the station people still go to the toilet, in fact I think deliberately because it isn't so shaky. The result is that everything goes straight through onto the tracks between the worn rails. When the train pulls out and everyone has waved off their relatives and friends, there are always a couple of clumps of what were the best available meals in the Railway Refreshment Rooms (RRR on our silverware). My job is to walk along the track between the rails with an old biscuit tin cut in half on a stick in one hand and a straw broom in the other and brush the steaming stuff off the ground.

This job is literally at the bottom of the barrel. I look like a bandit with a kerchief around my nose and mouth, scooping shit along the longest platform in nearly the world. Workers on the platform look down on me. Well, workers may not be the right word, but a junior temporary permanent station attendant is not as glamorous as it sounds. Taillight is a shunter and tells the other guys to lay off me and let me get on with the jobs.

Needless to say, I don't jump out of bed the next day to go to work. Then again, neither does anyone on the NSWGR payroll. I'm better off than a lot of guys my age. Some parents have sent them off to get a summer job and then charged them rent and board. They're lucky to break square.

* * *

Mum is discharged from Kenmore although Dr Tooth notes her prognosis is very doubtful. Dad drives up the Hume Highway in his EJ Holden with sheepskin dashboard, seat covers and steering wheel. A winking Jesus hangs from the rear vision mirror. They listen to 2GL Goulburn, 2WG Wagga and 2AY Albury on the way back. Mum's handbag brims with bottles of Antabuse, Amitriptylline, Fergon and Sparine.

It's boiling hot. It makes you very thirsty, being surrounded by sheep shagpile in the sun, even at 80 mph with the side windows open and angled to blow the hot shimmering air into your face.

Mum takes to bed for a few days to recover. Life is back to abnormal.

* * *

I've got a lot to look forward to: Georgina's visit, Christmas, New Year and university—whatever that is. My cousin Tom is doing law by correspondence. People can trust a lawyer who gets his licence by mail but I'd think twice before I let a doctor do surgery if he got his MD by correspondence. A law office seems up compared to the train tracks and I'm still not sure what doctors do, except it involves blood and body parts.

When I tell Mum and Dad about Georgina you'd think I'd announced that I'd done a murder. It makes Mum feel a million years old. She reaches inside the sleeve of her cardigan for the ever-present hankie. Dad blushes and says Greek you say. I explain that Greeks are Catholics, only darker. She can sleep in Katherine Ann's room, Mum helpfully suggests. My eyes meet Dad's but there is little else to say.

Mum is now making a good fist of her freedom, helping out in the bar and keeping an eye on Mrs Westie in the kitchen. She's taking the Antabuse and drinking loads of tea when the thirst comes upon her. In fact it's Mum who arranges for me to have the week off while Georgina is down. Dad doesn't think it'll matter as the NSWGR won't know I'm missing. But it's summer and the work will only pile up waiting for me when I get back. I'll be knee deep in it.

I can't sleep the night before Georgina is to arrive. My heart has been on hold since I left Sydney. Interestingly, my hand also has been on hold. Before I met Georgina I was in the process of writing a self-abuse manual with 100 new positions. Now I'm saving myself up.

Ever since a Chemistry class in fourth year, when my eyes first met cobalt blue in the test tube held by Porky Plunkett, I've known what I was looking for in the eyes of a lover. Georgina's are like sea-worn grottoes hidden behind her high cheekbones and noble nose. In room 17 the bedsheets twist around me like sails in a storm. Popovic the barber gets me a condom which I keep in the Gideon Bible next to the bed. Dad thought it was too good to be true when they gave boxes of bibles away free to hotels. He thought about bumping up the prices for the rent. Amazingly they were knocked off at a greater rate than the towels by our mainly pagan clientele. I guess that's what the Gideons were hoping for. It was a bit like Brer Rabbit: once they stole the bible, tucked it under their farside arm and walked out the front door as cool as could be, there wasn't much they could do but read it. There wasn't a big market for second-hand bibles at Batrouney's Auction House because everybody had one, had read one or had seen the movie at the Regent.

Mum puts a statue of Our Lady of Fatima on the bureau and empties half of Katherine Ann's wardrobe in readiness for Georgina. In my room, I roll up the poster of Raquel Welsh and put up the picture of six bulldogs playing poker. Otherwise room 17 is in a very high state of readiness, down to the Ginger Meggs throw carpet. I unplug the overhead Osram and put red cellophane over the bedside lamp. No wonder I can't sleep. The place is a sex trap.

I got my driving licence the old-fashioned way. Dad arranged for one of the young cops to come by the pub, pick me up and take me around the block then have a couple of schooners when we got back. He handed me the paperwork. Don't have a prang for six months. The least he could have done was let me help drive the car around the block.

But now I've got the keys of the Holden with door to door shagpile, push-button radio, cup-holders for the drive-in and a blanket in the boot. I motor up Smollett Street in fits and starts with my elbow out the window like I know what I'm doing. The Station Master spots me at the station. Whatcha doin here? You gotta week off. Miss the shit-kickin do you? Do you? Do you? All the shunters laugh with him. He's the Station Master of the Universe and I am the station slave.

The Spirit is late so I check myself in the huge yellowing mirror in the waiting room. Perfect. Not a hair in place. I manage the just-shagged look pretty well for a virgin. The cure is just around the corner at Culcairn and closing fast.

Georgina has spent her whole life in Sydney and has travelled to Europe and the old country. At the top of her upper arm is the international sign of travel, the round smallpox inoculation scar, which people in Peter Stuyvesant ads have, and migrants at Bonegilla. What will she make of Albury, where a pleasure craft is a tractor tyre at the Weir, where Greeks are known for cafés and the traffic lights have to be turned off to avoid pile-ups? Why have I invited her here where there's nothing to do but each other?

I fear she'll meet someone on the train and fall in

love and take the Spirit through to Melbourne with her new GPS First Eleven, First Fifteen, School Captain, Interschool Champion, Debating Captain on his way to his first tour of duty in Vietnam. The heart is a tortured priest. Part of you wants to cry Enough! and part wants to be a martyr. Mind you, the work on the tracks has given me a bit of a tan. I look a bit outdoorsy if not rugged. She'll be putty in my hands.

My mood swings from black to blue and back again. Love is waiting for the Spirit of Progress with your ear on one track, hoping to feel the vibrations and avoid the work piling up. It's coming. It's coming!—before I leapfrog onto the platform and cross my arms, resuming my trademark carefree casual couldn't-care-less calculated lean against the wall.

This is the real thing. A week of push-ups on top of a folded-out *Playboy* has brought me to the peak of condition.

Love Comes
to Town

She's got duck's disease says Dad. What? Her arse is too close to the ground. She may be short, but you know good things come in small boxes. Wink wink. Georgina and Dad get on like a house on fire. Mum immediately sees the torch I hold for Georgina is in safe hands. No one is going to get their fingers burnt yet. Women know women better than us. We take them at face value, especially if it's pretty. Women know themselves better than that. Mum is friendly as can be and can't show off Georgina's made-up bed and table quickly enough. She takes her under her wing, which is about where Georgina comes up to.

We all settle down in front of the television in the lounge although it's nine o'clock in the morning. Television is new to Albury, at least in people's homes. We even have our own station, and the family loves to watch even if it's only the test pattern. We chat during the ads. Since television came I think they'll have to rename living rooms all over Australia.

Georgina is full of opinions. Not in a stuck-up way, but there isn't a subject she doesn't know which side to take and why. Mum and me are made of a different stock. We can see two sides at once. There isn't an opinion we can't see an equal argument for the opposite of. I don't always agree with what Georgina says but besides keeping that to myself I thrill at the force and fire with which she espouses her views. It isn't her views I admire but the strength of them.

We have breakfast brought upstairs on a tray by Mrs Westie who wants to give Georgina the once over herself. She nods to me, impressed. Mum is asking what we plan to do, as if what I'm planning to do needs any planning. Charles—Georgina always calls me Charles— told me about this spot on the Murray where nobody goes. Cough cough. I have to interrupt because it's a renowned skinny-dipping venue and the whole thing might be misconstrued. There's the Monument, Norieul Park, the Weir and Mates window I explain. She smiles sideways like a child's see-saw. It's really bewitching and beautiful, pushing one of her cheeks right up until one eye is nearly closed. I love making her laugh just to see that eye crush tight.

The Hood himself towers over Georgina although he's only eight years old. But there's no doubt that Peter, John, The Hood and Katherine Ann all look up to Georgina. They can't believe I have a girlfriend, let alone this spitfire in black leather who makes them laugh and blush and feel important all at the same time. Nevertheless, she's so full on and strong we're all secretly a little afraid of her. Even Dad. He hasn't seen a T-shirt with a message on it before. NO CON-SCRIPTION is the gentlest inscription Georgina has among the T-shirts she's packed. Everybody's eyes are immediately drawn to the writing on her chest and the way it seems to move when she walks, like a blanket on a shared waterbed.

Georgina can't wait to pull a beer and before lunch everyone in the hotel is in love with her. We can't believe she's never eaten a counter lunch before, and after Mrs Westie's haricot chops in their own sauce we know she never will again.

Dad throws me the car keys and Georgina and I are singing Yellow Submarine down Dean Street before parking on Monument Hill for the long-awaited pash. After a couple of hours I sense we aren't alone. It must be Armistice Day because the car is surrounded by all these old guys in khaki woollen army uniforms look-ing in the windows as silent as snipers. We jump out of the seats believing they're the War dead buried under the Monument come to life. How long have they been there Georgina screams. But they aren't doing any harm and we're probably doing them a lot of good.

The skin around our mouths is all red in the rear vision mirror and the interior smells of our leather coats which must have been rubbing against each other for hours. We leave the Monument in a cloud of red dust. The old army men look at us as if we're leaving them behind enemy lines. But we don't feel too bad. They fought for the right to do what we've just been doing.

There's a bend in the river at Woomargama where the water slows down to a crawl, where the sand has built up over the years to form a kind of beach and thick surrounding bush provides cover for homeless lovers. I won't tell her where I'm taking her but when we arrive I think she already knew. The sun is over Wagga Wagga by now. The cackle of kookaburras is so loud you'd think there was a newsreel playing nearby. Georgina twirls and twirls in her boots on the sand near the water. I have the tartan blanket out of the boot and on the beach in the blink of an eye.

Georgina wants to swim. But we don't have our cossies I say. It's a lucky thing human sexual relations isn't a leaving certificate subject because I'd fail for sure. You first, I say, lying down on one elbow. Her tight black polo-necked skivvy gets stuck over her head with her arms in the air. She can't see and dares not move. I can see and it's magic. She's covered entirely in skin except for an elastic beige Berlei bra packed to bursting with even more skin. Despite her calls for help I can't move. So she twirls and twirls blindly and her breasts fly around like twin slingshots. They circle her as the wooden ponies circle on a carousel. If I could move I would reach out and undo the clips at the back and free them. Fly away. Fly away. You are free.

She finally throws the skivvy at me with a You aren't much help and undoes her bra by herself. Her breasts remain at attention while she wriggles out of her black jeans and white panties. She has more life in her than I have ahead of me. She dives under the water silkenly like a platypus and emerges with her hair draped across her face. This is better than TV. I could watch her all afternoon but she insists I join her. Cold water from 600 feet below the Hume Dam does not show a young man at his best nude-wise. Although strangely it makes Georgina's nipples stick out like the ends of long balloons. She stands in the water to her knees, her arms crossed over her chest, her pubic hair the shape of a traffic Yield sign pointing towards the water.

I run awkwardly into the river with both hands over my groin as if she won't notice that I need only one. There's a very good reason why the Eskimos didn't invade the Americas like the English and Spanish, why they don't rule the world in castles of ice bricks. When you're so fucking cold that your balls retract into the chest cavity, your face turns the colour of your eyes and the contents of your nose hang like icicles, your flight or fight instinct plays no part. It is really just plain frozen. I bet they all weed into the Yellow River before Chairman Mao took his swim.

Georgina breaks a chip of ice off the end of my nose. Her breasts float in front of her like crayfish pots. Blue veins criss-cross her chest in search of higher ground. We inch towards each other before embracing for warmth not lust. We kiss while I keep one eye open for water snakes trying to spoil the moment. I reckon it's too cold for them, but the tiger snake is a cold-hearted creature who'd love a bit of Greek for a change. Then I'd have to suck the poison out. Hopefully it would be a sharp-eyed tiger. The tiger is the most venomous in the world and the only antidote is kept in the Albury Base Hospital miles away. They're impossible to see in the water because their scaly skins are the colour of dappled running water. The first symptom of a tiger snake bite is sudden death.

I don't want to scare Georgina but I do want to get out of the fucking freezing water so I gently enquire if she's heard of the local tiger snake. We move much more quickly than we had been.

By the banks of the mighty Murray River I hold her in my arms brrring on Dad's tartan blanket. Our fingers feel each other's goosebumps like Braille. We give each other love bites in secret places, under the armpits, on the bottom cheeks. I try the scalp but Georgina says it hurts. We make like not love, deep deep like on the blanket on the banks until the bull ants march up. The angry red bull ant is the sworn enemy of bathers on blankets on the banks of the mighty Murray. It's nature's contraceptive.

The sun is way past Wagga Wagga when we drive out over the dirt roads with wet hair in licks on our faces, rubbing each other's leather coats for warmth. We haven't gone all the way but Woomargama's not far from it. We have the week ahead and the world at our feet, if only I can get my own out of each other's way.

* * *

Mum is in one of her mothering moods, as if making up for lost time. If she had her way we'd be in our pyjamas and off to bed straight after dinner. Separate beds. I feel embarrassed by the way she treats us like children. It takes a lot of whining about my job, how I've left school now and it's only eight o'clock and still light before we're allowed to walk up Dean Street. In a way I hate her like this. It's better when we set our own rules while she lies helpless in bed with the brandy and the pills scattered over the floor.

Dean Street at night is the crossroads of the world. Nearly every make and model of car is parallel parked there, and the front window lights of Albury's busiest stores bathe the footpaths in red and yellow until ten sharp, when no God-fearing person would be on the streets anyway. The street lights go off and Dean Street is as black as the bush except for the headlights of cars going up and down, up and down. Mayor Cleaver Bunton keeps the city's budget under his tight-fisted control. Over the river the city of Wodonga blazes all night like Sodom, attracting all the riffraff and new businesses.

The Hume Weir Café trades for travellers in the dark, and Fonts Famous Fish Café serves battered redfin and chips to the famished drunks of the Globe, the Albion, the George, the New Albury and even Nana's Pastoral Hotel. The booths at the Hume Weir Café spill over with teeming teenage thrillseekers. Hardly anyone is watching Homicide on the chestnut television over the counter with the squirrely aerial Scotchtaped in place.

Taillight has taken up with the wrong crowd who will lead him on the road to ruin according to Aunt Faith. The wrong crowd have parked their bikes in clusters at the kerb outside the café. Harleys and BMWs and the new Japanese bikes which would not have been allowed to park at the RSL carpark. Lest we forget means they never will forget at the RSL. The wrong crowd all wear leathers and are called bodgies by others and Hell's Angels by each other. Their jackets have Hell's Angels Albury painted in red on their backs. The wrong crowd don't need anyone else. They have each other. Chicks in leather ride on the back of bikes all the way out to the Weir and, as rumour has it, are shared among members. I tut-tut with Georgina at this but secretly think of saving for a bike. It's just the way the phrase Having their way with them sounds.

Taillight spots us and walks like the man from Twenty Thousand Leagues Under the Sea over to our booth. Georgina. Taillight. Taillight. Georgina. He looks me in the eye. I'm not called that any more. I'm Barry the Bastard now. Why, I ask, do they call you Barry? Good one Charlie, as he sits down next to Georgina and puts his whiskey-enriched soft drink bottle on the table. He has packets of NoDoz in his pockets. The wrong crowd keep looking over at us, including the dagger-eyed skinny tart known as The Bike. I don't think it's for the same reason as my mate at school.

Taillight, I mean Barry the Bastard's group are going out for a ride to the Weir. Come with us. Georgina is all for it. There's much to learn about her. Mum's expecting us, I explain. Barry the Bastard gives me one of Those Looks. The wrong crowd don't take much notice of their mums' curfews.

Georgina holds Barry's left hand and looks at where his little finger had been before it was caught between two train carriages he was shunting. He's got a long way to go before he catches up with armless Ernie Carpenter.

The boys and girls in the other booths look up from their milkshakes with two sharing straws as if we're consorting with the enemy. These boys wear long white socks to just below their knees and checked seersucker shorts and striped shirts. Bus timetables poke out of their top pockets. Georgina asks Barry the Bastard about the Ryan hanging, due in a few months. He's against all hanging unless it's cops.

I tap my wrist, indicating the time. We've hardly

touched our cinnamon toast, but I don't want Mum going off her tree when we get home. Georgina thinks we're normal so far, I believe. We're passing for human.

I pay in coins from the bottom of my trousers and wander out to a dark Dean Street. We walk with her arms around the top of my legs and my arms angled behind her, resting on her hip. Dean Street is as dead as a doornail. We own the footpaths. I show her my Albury. We kiss under the awnings outside Adams Funeral Parlour, in front of Brady's Hotel, on the steps of the Civic Theatre—anywhere I can put her on a higher plane so that I don't do my back in from stooping over.

We come into the pub through the back entrance. I recognise Dad's voice instantly. It's party time in the old saloon tonight. Mum is all mothered out and has taken to a shandy on her stool behind the bar, talking to one of the customers. I order two squashes, straight up. Georgina shows her skill on the pool table and there's no want of instructors, leaning over her like praying mantises, looking over their shoulders, showing off to the others. Captain Jack Saunders (retired) coughs loudly to restore some sense of order. No one hears him at first. He coughs louder. Still nothing. Finally he coughs until green phlegm comes uncontrollably out of his mouth and hits his fist before falling onto the matching green felt pool table. Jack Shiebs pulls out a giant dirty handkerchief from his tobacco-infested pocket and wipes the offending smear deeply into the felt.

Everyone is jam-packed into the pool room. The front bar is dimmed so passersby and police will be fooled into thinking we're closed. The inventor of the pool table didn't count on forty or fifty patrons packed around it in a room the size of a toilet where you can't see the nose on the end of your face because of the cigarette smoke. There's a high chance of hostilities breaking out with an elbow in the eye here or a pool stick in the eye there. Dad has to hose things down from time to time.

The Captain retires to his quarters with a flagon of port to rue his lost authority. We have a swig or two of beer when Dad isn't looking and it's Knees Up Mother Brown in no time, in no time at all. Mum has given up hope of getting us to bed and it's a wonderful thing to see that the Greeks and the Irish have so much in common. Georgina is more of a show-woman than I would have guessed and the back bar breaks into a chorus of Hava Nagila Have Another Gila until after midnight. I know it's time for bed when Dad gets That Look and puts his arm around me and begins his favourite lines of Kipling's If:

If you can fill the unforgiving minute
    With sixty seconds' worth of distance run,
  Yours is the Earth and everything that's in it,
    And—which is more—you'll be a Man, my son!

Mum comes over, all awash in mascara, reaching for the bar cloth to blow her nose. My own face is alive with the embarrassment but Georgina is beaming at me so much that one eye is completely shut and the tell-tale red blotches break out on her lower neck and upper chest that I later learn to watch out for as they portend sexual interest, like red rashes to a bull. The snooker stick is bigger than she is. She has to reach up to chalk the tip. In her long black leather coat, feet astride and snooker stick in one hand, the other on her hip with the cigarette smoke as still as fog against the yellow light, she beckons this boy who needs no beckoning. We ascend the stairs while Kipling gives way to Killarney and I'll take you home again Kathleen, to where the fields are fresh and green, and we make for Room 17.

Georgina is small but we're the same height lying down on my single bed. Dry-rooting was a full dress rehearsal for this. We take each other's clothes off like tailors and drape them over the spare bed. The moon is the size of one of Dad's toenail clippings so the only light that comes through the gauze is the red running writing of neon light from the roof that spells out Waterstreets Hotel.

Our bodies look sunburnt against the bottom sheet while our feet push the top sheet, blankets and bedcover into the gap between the mattress and the end of the bed. Her hair smells of Philip Morris, Pall Mall and Rothmans filters from the back bar but the body still has the scent of the cool water of the Mighty Murray. We cover each other in kisses. The bed creaks with our caresses. Just as I find a part of her I love better, another part appears to demand my immediate attention, and so it goes as I work my way around her like a game of Monopoly.

Through the other window above our heads you can see the long white needle of the War Memorial standing guard over the sleepless city. Behind us the sounds of shunting trains in the distance are interrupted by the occasional long road transport taking the short cut by Smollett Street at speed. The bulldogs look down on us, frowning in disapproval over their cards.

Now she lies on top of me; fingers interlocked in mine, outstretched as if on the Cross, lips locked, my cock clutched firmly by her thighs, she sails me to shore. Slowly she releases me and pulls her knees up on either side and jockeys up to my chest, sitting on me as her white white breasts threaten to avalanche and bury me breathless in my bed. It's a moment that needs no words. My hands leave her breasts without support, she firms her grip on me and we turn quickly like a rotisserie and I'm on her and suddenly in her. I am in heaven which is why I think she's crying out my name when she says Oh my God, oh my God. I can't tell if it's pleasure or pain but her long fingers grab my back as if she's hanging on for dear life. The Oh my Gods get louder and louder and I lose concentration and before too long I'm mixing my own Oh my Gods with

Charles Waterstreet

her Oh my Gods and it's Oh my God oh my God oh my God drowning out the drones of lorries and the clunks of shunted carriages. By dawn I know love is more than masturbating in company.

Red Sails in the Sunset

The summer sun is cruel to sleeping lovers, startling them awake into the glare of another scorched day so unlike the night before. Georgina quickly grabs my best T-shirt and flees to the made-up bed in Katherine Ann's room and messes it up till it looks exhausted from the tossing and turning.

I have my hands behind my head against the pillow, smiling the self-satisfaction of the truly unsophisticated. Georgina's 4711 fills the air like Aerogard. I bring my fingers to my nose as if they're a delicate cheese. I can't believe what's in front of my eyes. My hands are covered in blood. They look like they belong to a Filipino faith healer. I jump out of bed thinking there must have been a murder. The sheet is soaked in it in the middle. I check my bum for blood and my body for bullet holes. Contrary to what the poets say, ignorance is not all bliss and it's minutes before I work out what has occurred. I sit on the side of the bed gazing into the middle. A wave of something weird overtakes me. At first it is the realisation that Georgina must have been a virgin. I know I was, but not in my wildest dreams did I think that anyone who had dated the whole back line of Waverley Firsts would be.

Just as I'm mentally notching the bedpost with my knife, signifying the first of many, wondering whether the bedhead will be big enough to carry all the future notches, I suddenly realise that she must be doing the same. It wasn't the Firsts that took her but we are the firsts with each other. Dad told me that you never forget your first lover. I asked him who it was. He coughed into his hand and said he'd never really got her name. But this is different. Georgina and I are biblically bound together in love, in her blood.

Then I snap out of it quick smart. In a wild panic I strip the sheet off the bed and throw it out the window to dry in the cruel summer sun. I pull down the window frame hard to keep it in place. I wash her off me in the boarders' shower, rubbing the sides of my nails with the washcloth down to the quick. Once I've cleaned the scene of the grime and stand with the top half of my body bent at right angles under the low shower-head trickling precious drops of the Mighty Murray out at full pelt, I close my eyes and feel the beat of my body, alive and alarmed. I can't wait to see Georgina. All my life I've been an addict in search of a drug.

Now I've found her. I am hooked. Hopefully she's a drug in search of an addict. I feel I can read her mind from the boarders' showers. She is thinking exactly the same things as me. How can I tell her thoughts from mine? How can I be sure they are her thoughts? They could be mine.

If this is love, give me more. Confusion is a small price to pay. Is she thinking of Cranky O'Brien now? Or was she thinking of him last night? I'm getting jealous of her future lovers as well. True love means making love with one eye over your shoulder making sure the next lover isn't too close. It is driving me mad, a direction and destination I'm probably heading for. Last night flashes before me like the small plastic slide-box Popovic the Barber sold on the side. My body beats so hard I believe I might have a body attack.

Captain Jack Saunders (retired) raps his brown fingers on the boarders' bathroom door. Hey you in there. I need to get to the latrine. Quick smart. At the double.

I open the door wrapped in a Waterstreets Hotel towel.

Sorry Charlie, but nature calls, time and tide wait for no man; I need to point percy at the porcelain.

Sure Jack. It's all yours.

He has the *Border Morning Mail* under his arm and a thick pencil for the crossword. He knows how to fill the lonely hours before the front bar opens.

I dress and pray I look like the same person Georgina liked so much last night. She glows and glistens at the top of the stairs like an apparition. Her wet hair combed back like a Riverina ladies' man, her face free of make-up or blush, white and bright, her neck red with the nervous rash that tells the onlooker the very thing he wants to know. She still loves him. We blush in sync and hug before joining the boarders for breakfast.

Don't you love the smell of ironing? We're passing the linen room. I live for it. We giggle. Until she told me I never noticed the smell of ironing. I feel now I can't live without it.

I can hear my parents talking in the flat. I have been on a long journey, and travelled the distance from between my mother's legs to the place between my lover's legs.

* * *

Through breakfast and the early morning we read the papers and lounge about in the secret world of luxuriating lovers, where any effort at all is too much and every word a tantalising taunt. The kids are off at school and Mum walks around the flat a little the worse for wear. She carries a feather duster for balance.

Georgina has heard all about the Hume Weir Dam and wants to see it for herself. Mum says we have to visit the relatives, which in a Catholic family like ours will take most of the day because there's so many aunties and uncles. Cousins we can cover tomorrow.

Grandma Waterstreet runs her own pub down the road. We aren't plate throwers like the Georges but what we lack in passion we make up for in numbers.

Just as I'm about to tell her about the extended family history, Dad comes bounding up the stairs three at a time. Look out the beer garden he laughs. Georgina and I look at each other and make for the boys' room which overlooks the beer garden. There are half a dozen old tippies (Totally and Permanently Incapacitated pensioners) throwing rocks at the window of room 17. They are as angry as ants, picking up stones that have bounced off the bricks and throwing them again. When I lean out, I can see the sheet from my bed flapping about in the breeze. Why in heaven's name are they throwing rocks at my room? Dad doubles over and you can barely hear him splutter out They think it's the Japanese flag!

As it turns out, the Greeks have a wedding ceremony where they deliberately put the bridal sheet out the window to prove she was a virgin, but try to tell that to a gang of drunken tippies. Toyotas are still barred from the car park at the RSL when even Volkswagens are allowed in.

We make love at every tourist destination in the Albury district. It leaves a lot of time for other things. Love is weird. I want to show Georgina off and keep her to myself all at the same time. She takes to love-making like a duck to water. It becomes hard for this young man to keep it up. Popovic the Barber, Is der anything else?, helps out with a tube of Stud 100, a guaranteed stay-hard cream. Popovic pops it into a huge brown bag which he crunches down to a size still too big for my hands to hold. Taillight put me onto the Stud 100. Not, he says, spitting onto the footpath to his left, that I need it son.

In the love-nest that Room 17 has become, I put the tube in the top drawer with the Goanna Oil, Mentholatum Deep Heat, cod liver oil, Waterburys Compound, nutmeg and other love potions we are starting to experiment with.

In the twilight of afternoon I sit astride Georgina's stomach, rubbing the Vaporub deep into her chest lest she catch a cold. Her breasts hang at each side like beanbags. I know exactly what she needs. I reach for the cream and rub handfuls over my all too eager untrusting steed. After years of pleasing and pleasuring myself in the shortest possible time after lights out, it's little wonder that adapting to the rigors of relationship rigidity needs some help. Suitably stiffened, I plunge the pink sword into its juicy scabbard.

The screaming sounds orgasmic at first. I smile confidently to myself. She is soon screaming and thrashing about like a Banshee. I believe that God has given me this gift. But she screams and rushes out the door towards the flat and into the bathroom. Georgie. Georgie! I cry. I understand. Before I can put on my jeans the skin on my cock flares bright red and an incredible surge of pain makes its way towards my brain. Instinctively checking the tube of cream now under the bed, I note that it is Mentholatum Deep Heat, not Popovic's Permanent.

Although this explains much it does little to cool either of us down. Our ardour falls at the same rate as burnt skin off our genitals. I offer to kiss it better. No go. Twilight is a dangerous time in a room without artificial lighting. We are the first sexual burn-outs of our generation.

* * *

Georgina takes Albury by storm. She speaks to the Fonts at their Famous Fish Café in Greek. Mrs Font and she compare tit size. Con has long stopped complaining of Toula's low-slung dresses which turn committed meat-eaters into fish lovers just for the view. Nana sees good bone structure. The Aunts want to know exactly how close the Greek Orthodox Church is to the Catholics. Same costumes, same rituals, but with beards.

Albury girls are slightly suspicious of a woman who doesn't drink beer but wine. Like the winos, they whisper. Everywhere she goes, if she doesn't make friends she makes a fuss never forgotten. Larger than my life. I love her zest, her vitality, her juiciness. We play every jukebox in town. I can't keep my hands off her. We drive to Deniliquin and drive each other to distraction.

If we were dusted for fingerprints, there wouldn't be a square inch without one.

The car nearly turns over at Dead Man's Curve on the Wagga Wagga road. Her hair spreads like a mop over my lap, I can't find the gearstick as my eyes close as I come. It's impossible. Nature does not allow the eyes to stay open during sneezes, seizures or sex. Don't drive during any of them.

We collect the bones and skulls of horses, sheep, goats and excitedly maybe human remains from Uncle Jim's farm. The boot of Dad's Holden looks like The Phantom's Skull Cave. We vow to keep everything as mementoes of the day in the country. A housemaid throws them out before Georgina leaves.

I love her skin. It covers her whole body. What enormous luck. We feel sorry for others who don't have us.

Georgina was born on Christmas Day which makes her like Jesus a Capricorn. She knows astrology like I once knew the back and front of my hand. She says that Cancers and Capricorns are not compatible. I want to change my star sign by deed poll to something compatible. It's not that easy. Are you sure I ask. There are tropics that circle the world named after our signs, and Henry Miller books. We are star-uncrossed lovers. I explain how I must have been premature. In many things, she hisses, certainly immature, with a wave of her hand. She knows all my buttons and never has her fingers off them. But she has her soft spots that I never have my fingers off either. Fuck the star signs. Surely we are the exceptions to their rule.

She sends secret postcards to Katie in Sydney all the time. I check the mail out every day to make sure she isn't writing to Cranky on the side.

* * *

We spend her last night in watching television with the whole family. Dad settles into his favourite couch with the fold-out footrest and fold-back headrest. He looks like an astronaut at take-off. We all fight over which of the two channels we'll watch. AMV4 is the best because it doesn't have as much snow as Shepparton's GMV6. They mostly show the same shows except for local news. Shepparton has fruit fly plagues and Albury floods and fires.

The Hood insists on sitting with his face almost touching the cellophane covering the television screen because, he says, it tickles. An eight-year-old head in front of Homicide at a crucial plot point is enough to make Dad thrash about looking for the lever to touch down and clip The Hood's ears, but he can never find it. Paul or John do it for him.

Mum sips a beer on the couch. Georgina and I cuddle like refugees on the last train out of Casablanca. We make love the night through, with the right tube in my hand.

* * *

Dad drives us to Culcairn when inevitably we miss Georgina's train back to Sydney. I don't see her again for the whole of the summer but we almost pay for the coaxial cable with our phone calls.

The summer is one long heatwave after another. The Station Master of the Universe orders me down onto the tracks immediately after each train pulls out lest the pong drive everyone even madder than they are with the heat. The City Council built a brand new swimming pool for the people of North Albury but it opens before they could agree on a name. The North Albury Lavington Olympic Swimming Centre is a bit of a mouthful says Alderman Luff. The North Albury Apex Club puts on a fundraiser for the Albury Sub-normal Children's Training Centre. They need portable air conditioners and water coolers. The teachers and children are perspiring the days away without blinds and with no ventilation. They can't use fans because the kids keep losing their fingers when they poke at them.

A Wodonga girl wins the Zhivago-look quest and a Wagga lass takes third place of $30-worth of Scamp underwear by Hickory.

Boundaries are being broken down all over the world. Frisbees have found their way to Norieul Park and you can't put your head up quickly from the towel without risk. The *Border Morning Mail* runs a series of articles on the frisbee phenomenon. Pop stars collapse all over Australia from 'overwork'. The outpatients departments of hospitals are run off their feet on Christmas Day with an epidemic of chokings on the new one cent pieces in plum puddings. Albury men beat the heat with the latest fad for patterned cotton shorts and long white socks.

Christmas dinner is a corker. Pineapple Porphyry Pearl flows like floodwater. Mum has won a pair of real turkeys in a raffle at the Commercial Club and Dad delegates Captain Jack Saunders (retired), who delegates Jimmy B, to deliver the coup de grace. With a couple of dozen quick blows of the axe Jimmy B has their heads off and most of their body parts scattered from one end of the back yard to the other. Jimmy B fought the Nips up north but says he's a bit rusty with turkeys. Mrs Westie plucks the bits Jimmy B brings inside in a mop bucket.

I get about a dozen tie and hankie sets for Christmas. Sixteen is such an awkward age to buy for. I give them to Dad, who is set for life tie and hankie wise.

Dad decides to charge the boarders extra for Christmas dinner, to balance the books. More like the bookies cracks Mum. It works a treat. No one pays, but it's chalked up in the Black Loan Book in the drawer in the front bar. It reads like the Who's Who of Waterstreets Hotel. You wouldn't believe who owes money. And for how long.

Mum and Dad fall asleep at the table before pudding,

which means the trip to the Weir is off. They wake in a flurry looking for cigarettes and matches. They go upstairs for a quick snooze before the trip to Nana's. Christmases are definitely getting longer, I hear, as they mount the stairs delicately.

* * *

Georgina rings after Christmas to tell me that she's missed her period. I phone every day to check on her and sweat blood myself. I fear I'll have to keep working under the Station Master of the Universe all my life, picking up after the intercity trainsetters leave Albury. I feel too young to be a teenager let alone a parent. My child will probably grow up to be older than me. How can I tell my parents I'm going to be one of them?

McIntosh the postman comes into the bar one morning while I'm helping out Dad. He leaves the usual bundle of mail in a rubber band and flicks a telegram along the green linoleum towards me. It's good news Charlie. Congratulations: you're not going to be a daddy after all. What, I scream, how the hell do you know? It makes me really angry for a while. The envelope with the telegram hasn't even been licked to keep it shut. He's out the door before I unfold the telegram. It reads Red Sails in the Sunset Love Georgina.

There are no secrets to the postmen of the Border City. The phone operators at the PMG listen to every conversation you ever have. Sometimes, if you're stumped for a word, they'll break in with it. Most people in Albury speak in code on the phone.

The Post Master General makes a packet from the love poems I carefully copy out and send to Georgina, pretending I made them up. Keats and Yeats only need a bit of an update and a tweak here and there to become a Waterstreet. I cross out words to give the air of creative process before folding the page and placing it in the blue stamped hotel envelope with the Queen's head stamp pre-licked and paid for. I blush beetroot when Georgina tells me on the phone that she wants to publish one in a magazine. I come over all shy and say it's private, for her eyes only.

Lying on the line takes a whole new technique. I'm a natural. Sometimes I write out entire conversations before I phone. We talk the text to my heart's content. The PMG has it all with the love letters and the long-distance telephone calls. Dad baulks at the bill when it comes in. Strictly speaking, love is not tax deductible.

* * *

On New Year's Eve in Dean Street scores of cars stall with their horns blasting and radios turned up full blast on 2AY's midnight countdown. The first local baby of the year, Miss 1967, is born on January 5th at the Wodonga District Hospital.

The next day Mum books into Kenmore for a rest.

She ran out of Antabuse at Christmas and has been slipping into old habits. The lemonade has disappeared from her shandies, fingers of brandy in a glass have become fists, and boxes of Relaxatabs fill the plastic kitchen tidy with the push-in lid. She speaks of Jesus and gibberish. She is not herself. She breaks all our hearts. Thank God Georgina is not here to see this.

Dad makes the familiar trip up the Hume Highway to Kenmore with Aunt Faith as muscle. With Mum away, he has Mrs Westie's tripe every day. When I query him about it on a Friday we fall into an ecclesiastical debate as to whether sheep's stomach lining is meat.

I stay out so late that there is just snow and static on the television whenever I get home. I team up with Danny Finn and Billy Purcell most nights. They were at St Patrick's with me before I went away. We drink milkshakes and beers in Dean Street, waiting for the movies to finish so we can ogle the girls. There's never a chance any one of us will score. It's the law of the borderland. They're gobsmacked when they hear about Georgina. I give them an earful every night.

I get paid in real decimal currency every fortnight at the railway. I cut up newspapers in the size of ten-dollar notes and wrap the real ones around them before pulling on a rubber band. My wad is the size of a jam tin. You should see the look on the girls' faces when I pull it out and peel one off to pay for the cinnamon toast.

Forrester's Beach

Georgina is beside herself on the phone but I can still hear her clearly. I'm sure that even if she hung up and kept talking I could hear her all the way from Sydney, she has a voice that can carry. Prime Minister Ky of South Vietnam is in Australia without getting her permission, and here he is calling the opposition leader Mr Calwell a communist. I feel I should contribute to the discussion as I called her and Dad is paying. They have very short names there, don't they? Do you think it's code?

Charlie, everything is not a joke. Ky wants the States to use nuclear weapons. On who? The Cong, North Vietnam and maybe China. It would start a nuclear war. I explain that Albury would be relatively safe and we could live in the beer cellar. She says I should be going down to Melbourne to help save Ronald Ryan who popeyed Premier Bolte wanted to hang to distract the voters from the lack of good roads and drainage.

I need to talk to her more, preferably in the nude, in bed, heart to heart. I can talk to Georgina for hours at a time. More precisely, I can listen to her for hours. I need to see her real bad, and discuss the Vietnam and missionary positions.

Dr Tooth discharges Mum within two weeks of her third admission to Kenmore on Amitriptylline, Antabuse and a new sedative, Mischloral, 10 ml to be taken at night. Dad drives her back to Albury without assistance. Mum is as bright as a button. He sings I'll take you home again Kathleen, to where the fields are fresh and green, to where you'll feel no pain, I will take you home again Kathleen.

* * *

The bottom has fallen out of my railroad job. It can't go on forever. The Vocational Guidance Bureau in the Civic Theatre building tests me at Mum and Dad's suggestion. Dad beams at my triple-figure IQ test result. He is convinced his side of the family gave me the gift to do sums.

The Vocational Guidance officer wears a cardigan although Albury is in the grip of a heatwave where the mercury is never below 100 during the day. He himself had been out of work since the school at which he was teaching closed down and he was mighty relieved to finally get this job giving vocational guidance. He has my test papers in front of him and is humming and hawing his way through them while I sit in shorts admiring my calves when I tense them. You have high 90s in both Arts and Science. Good. That means that you have high abilities in the writing side and in the scientific field.

I explain that that's why I'm here, because I'm going to do medicine but lately I've been thinking of law as I have a close cousin my age doing it at Albury by correspondence. I tell him I have a Commonwealth Scholarship in medicine which will pay me to go to Sydney University. I ask him what he thinks I should do.

With your science and your English skills there's a perfect job for you that would suit right down to the ground. I think I've done that at the railroad already, I say. No, he says, you can become a patent officer at the Patent Office. I haven't heard of that. What's that? It's a three-year tech course, you can do it here in Albury at the Albury Tech. Three years part-time. Then you get a job in a Patent Office assessing inventions and stuff, and writing them up in English.

I cross my fingers and promise to get back to him. I haven't loafed about at Waverley, sleeping in and playing sport all day for the last year, just to do a tech course in Albury.

* * *

Danny Finn and Billy Purcell are planning a motor trip up the Central Coast, past Sydney, in Danny's father's Finns the Carpet Kings Ford station wagon. The idea is to stop at caravan parks along the coast, sleeping in the back or hiring a caravan at the site. Between Albury and the Central Coast of New South Wales lies Georgina George, and where lies Georgina George lie I.

I bundy off from my junior temporary permanent station assistant job for the last time. The Station Master of the Universe says I'm throwing away a secure future without the necessity of work. Charlie, it's hard for a fool like me to fathom. I'll have to tell your father. He knows, and wants you to keep it open for my brothers. Okey dokey.

Mrs Finn packs Finns the Carpet Kings Ford station wagon like a tool kit. We'll never get everything out and back in without her. Although I've been for my driving licence, Finn and Purcell have major misgivings about my driving on the Hume Highway, which is four lanes wide in parts, two going and two coming. I can park in driveways and some beach roads.

Mum gets up to make me breakfast on the morning we leave. Dad has put a small kitchenette with a gas ring in the flat. Mum cracks three eggs into the pan and lays down two rashers next to them. It's the first meal she's cooked all for me. The kids are still asleep, Dad hasn't stirred except for the snoring like sawing and occasional lip quivers of expelled air. Sitting in the kitchenette at the Formica table with aluminium legs with knife and fork poised I feel like a real family, like Ricky Nelson or Beaver or one of My Three Sons. Mum seems fine but a little groggy, but not from the grog. The eggs look like singed doilies with burnt sticks of bacon. I eat it all up with toast soldiers.

I take one of Dad's big square leather pieces of luggage which I carry on my knees to Wollongong where Purcell has cousins in the dry cleaning business. Mum waves me off in an apron at the top of the stairs as I negotiate the bag a step at a time down and around the curling staircase.

I take a brown bank-wrapped bundle of 20-cent coins for the phone that was sitting in Dad's upstairs office shoulder to shoulder with other coin bundles. Dad calls them knuckledusters. I call Georgina from every telephone box between Albury and Wollongong. Costs me a fortune to stay in touch. I save the last coins to call Simmo. He's doing an insurance selling course. We'll catch up on my way back from the Central Coast. Grantie is working on the farm and The Bike has been sent overseas by his parents to see the world. It's the only place to see the rest of the world I explain to Simmo. See you.

Wollongong is like Wagga Wagga by the sea. Purcell's cousins can't put all of us up for the night so I go to Uncle Jack's on Campbell Street to sleep. We're the toast of Wollongong and are treated like royalty. I guess Wollongong doesn't get many visitors. They haven't seen three Albury lads out on the town in the Finns the Carpet Kings Ford station wagon before and we play up something fierce, telling jokes and drinking beer like it's lemonade. I ring the George residence late at night but when a sleepy and irritated gynaecologist answers I hang up.

In the morning Aunty Irene asks if I have a hangover. No I say, getting gingerly onto my high horse, it's the lag and crossing the time zones getting here. Uncle Jack says It's only 300 miles. It's relative.

Finn picks me up and we do a last lap of town before tackling the Bulli Pass and on to Sydney. We realise that we have no place to stay in Sydney, and have a booking at a caravan park just before The Entrance. I'll have to be quick with Georgina. Don't use the cream says Purcell. I regret telling him about that.

The station wagon has air-conditioning if you wind the windows all the way down, including the rear window. The smell of damp underfelt clings to the interior like mould. Finn fiddles with the tuning knob after leaving the Gong, testing the limits of 2WO and its Top Forty. More like 1940 says someone in the back seat where I'm sitting alone. Fifty miles out of Sydney, Ward Pally Austin breaks through occasionally as if we're a B29 returning to base after being shot up over Germany. He plays only hits and speaks Australian with an American accent. He says things like a-rick-a-poddie and a-fandoogalie. We've made the Big Smoke.

* * *

Georgina's parents' house has indented white columns outside forming a guard to the porch. The exterior is painted in discreet lavish tones, befitting their station in life. The front lawn has headless and armless statues on blocks as if advertising for spare parts to passing traffic. Finn and Purcell refuse to get out of the car. I haven't seen Georgina since we were almost parents ourselves so I blush when Dr George comes out the front door which has knobs the size of barbecue trays. He waves me in with his left hand. The little fingers of each hand have extraordinarily long nails. He must poke them out to the side during inspections like Aunt Faith drinking tea from a saucer.

I can hear Georgina's pitter patter from the back of the house, where the Georges have a below-ground swimming pool the colour of a grotto with jets of water spurting into the air around the sides and into the pool. Dr George built it after a heart scare and now does daily laps. It's about 15 feet long by 6 feet wide.

Georgina bounces off the carpet and onto my lips, wrapping her legs tightly around my shoulders. It's like Ashtons Circus I say when I finally have to come up for air after the liplock. Mrs George has prepared keftaris and stuffed olives and other Greek fare. There's enough to feed a small army. Finn and Purcell are fetched and after some initial poking and prodding we gobble it down.

Georgina has the red rash over her chest and neck. I eat with one hand and hold her hand with the other all through lunch. From time to time my foot rubs hers. Ouch that hurts. She's barefooted, while I have thick Hush Puppies. Sorry.

The Georges are for the war, but Georgina is a significant minority. It won't be long before the cutlery and plates are flying. I try changing the subject to the Ryan hanging, which leads to fist with fork banging and Hanging's too good for the bastard.

It's time to hit the road to Woy Woy which, I wink to Georgina, is right next to The Entrance. We kiss for ages. Her on the porch. Me on the lawn. We promise to stay longer when we return. I blow kisses out the window all the way down Gardiner's Road.

* * *

Forrester's Beach Caravan Park is alive with mosquitos at night. We spray each other's entire bodies, including under the arms, before jumping into the bedbunks of the Viscount caravan without wheels we've rented for the week. Leftover Christmas beetles barge into the glass windows of the caravan and lie upside down wriggling their eight legs in the air, opening and closing their wings for purchase. Finn says Georgina will never break her nose if she ever fell forward. Purcell isn't so sure. She's got a Roman nose, meaning all over the place. Oh piss off, I say, quick as a flash. I'm dying of lover's balls and sperm poisoning.

Finn has the bunk above me. He's heard about me

touching the monstrance on the bush telegraph all the way from Sydney. Before too long we're carrying out our own Black Mass in the Viscount. Jesus as Jatz crackers gets us going, and when we get to picking up the hosts from the Carmelites there's no stopping us. I like my Jesus in hi-fibre. Hi-fibre Jesus says Purcell like a television announcer. I want lo-cal Jesus because I'm on a diet and bread and meat are soooo fattening. The Viscount begins to rock on the bricks stacked under-neath. Is there a vegetarian Jesus for those who don't eat meat asks Finn. Exactly. How can you believe it is really Jesus and eat him if you're a vegetarian? Perhaps if they put out a nutty Jesus. But the nuts would still turn into Jesus's body. With my luck, I say, I'd get his foreskin. Yuck, this is 33 years older than the last Jesus I ate. There's a hair in my Jesus, sir. Sir, sir, I've got bum Jesus, can I have something down the leg? Poofter priests gobble down their Big Jesus like they're going down. Penis Jesus. Finn wants a Choctop Jesus. On a stick. Paddle Pop Jesus. On a cross. Jesus as snack food. Chomping Jesus. Triple decker Jesus. With the lot. Washed down with Gehrig's 66 sweet sherry. So fill-ing, so fulfilling. Limits Jesus—you won't feel like eating anything else. You'll be full of Jesus. Chewy Jesus— lasts all day until the next life. The Viscount shifts on the bricks as it rocks harder and harder. Jawbreaker Jesus. He'll never die. NoDoz Jesus. He'll keep you on your toes. Beer Jesus with a big head.

I think maybe we're going too far. Maybe, just

maybe, there is a God, frowning above the caravan park. No way. Iced Vo-vo Jesus. And on into the night. I feel sorry for non-Catholics who can't experience the hardcore thrill of full-frontal sacrilege. Good night. My hand. My lover.

* * *

We wake in our caravan on bricks still giggling, as if sleep was just a freeze-frame, and last night's conversation continues perfectly edited. Finn announces that it's Ash Wednesday so after a quick dip in the sea we make our way to the communal barbecue pit under a green fibro cover with hastily thumbed bitumen smeared across our foreheads. Other heads turn. Catholic campers quickly look away. Protestants think we're filthy, and frown so hard that Chinese characters like huts appear at the base of their foreheads, between their eyebrows.

We are perfect Christian Gentlemen. Brother Davy would have been proud. He wrote *The Christian Gentleman*, the bible for young Catholic men. He made us aware that too much beach makes us listless and disinclined to mental effort. He wrote that in some beach resorts persons offend good taste and moral decency by immodesty in dress in order to attract attention to themselves. Finn, Purcell and I have been on the lookout for these people from the time we got up. There are some likely suspects gathered in pairs, eating sausages, covered only in colourful batiks from the Far East. Finn drops his cutlery from time to time, checking for underwear. Brother Davy gives no insight as to finding out if women are wearing underwear. He's big on theory but hopeless in the field. My recent adventures in the skin trade with Georgina have awakened the explorer in me. I'm willing to ply the trade in further fields. I feel cocky in every sense of the word. But at the back of my mind, well, behind the bitumen smear, a sense of fear lurks that last night we went too far, that the First Commandment has a breaking point even though most of the rest of me doesn't believe in all that horseshit.

Tara and Sophie are from Cronulla, staying with their parents but eating of course at the farthest table away from them. They're going to university this year to study arts. Finn asks who their favourite painter is. Finn is following his dad into rug dealing. He's going to be the Carpet Prince. Purcell is going into government. Local government. He'll be working for Albury Council, adding up the water rates. The days of leaving your hose on in the garden for nothing are over.

We spread our towels out in the classic sunburst formation, heads in the middle and five points of bare feet stretched out like the Christmas star. The girls have their cigarettes, tissues, baby oils, matches, purses and magazines in the centre piled up with our paperbacks, Finn's transistor and a tube of zinc cream. Finn has to fiddle with the tiny dial as if performing a delicate brain operation until he gets 2GO which plays Mantovani, Mantovani and Mantovani.

Cronulla girls hang out in pairs and bikinis. The Albury boys' eyes dart about like pinballs, trying to take it all in but trying not to appear that way. Tara knows every Beatle's name, including their middle ones. Sophie covers Australian groups and knows all their covers. I tell the girls about The Loved Ones and their massive hit The Loved Ones. What's their name? The Loved Ones. Oh. What's their album? The Loved Ones. Oh. Their song? Loved Ones. Oh. Not much imagination there. I defend them as great and powerful and from Melbourne. I wish they could hear it but 2GO has as much chance of playing The Loved Ones as playing Guantanamera by the Sandpipers.

Tara says her dad has a long aerial in their caravan which we can hook up to Finn's transistor to pick up a Sydney station. Purcell and Tara sneak up and back holding about five yards of plastic-covered wire. Finn sticks the copper wire strands into his mouth and twists them with his tongue into a bunch. Years of carpet laying with tacks, he says. He fits it into the aerial hole and Tara and Sophie hold the red wire over their heads like lifesavers. Finn moves them about, turning the dial with a pair of finely tuned fingers. Suddenly we can hear Ward Pally Austin again, the DJ from America working his passage around the world from station to station. He wears all white trousers and shirt and hair straight from the bottle. He glows in the dark. He rules the airwaves and we're getting him live on Forrester's Beach—if only Tara and Sophie can keep their arms high in the air. The trannie isn't large and the girls can hardly hear it, so I replay to them what's being played. It's the Top 40 Countdown. Purcell plays his air guitar. I sing into my fist.

The girls' legs are starting to buckle and the reception is suffering. Finn barks orders to keep their spirits and arms up. After some reorganisation the trannie is placed on a sand castle facing exactly north-east and the wire lies like a long thin snake in the exact configuration arrived at after hours of nudging back and forth. We resume the classic starburst.

Sophie asks me about the future. I'm going to university. Doing what? Maybe law, or medicine. I haven't quite decided. You'd better hurry up, says Tara, or all you'll be doing is illegal abortions. We blush. Cronulla girls really do have mouths on them. My Mum and Dad run a pub in Albury. Unlimited beer. The girls perk up. Publicans have a bit of status up here with Cronulla chicks that is obviously underrated at home. I'm an exile in my home country town.

When I first hear my name over the radio it goes in one ear and out the other, like Mantovani. But then I hear it again. Ward Pally Austin is actually saying my name. Finn and Purcell stop in their tracks, although they're both lying down flat. Finn, who has known me all my life, says Is that you? I still can't believe what

I'm hearing. My name. Again and again. By Pally. Over 2SM. He says I'm to ring Uncle Jack in Wollongong.

Sophie says that maybe I've won the lottery. Yeah. I jump to my feet. None of us has money. I run to the caravan shop and ask if I can use their phone. I'll ring reverse charges. Promise.

Suddenly I'm speaking to Uncle Jack, who says The Good Lord relieved your mum of all her irresponsibilities this morning. She died in bed. Your dad found her. I'm very sorry. Get back to Sydney and come in my car with Aunty Irene and the rest back to Albury.

I walk slowly back to our towels. Everybody's staring at me. Mum doesn't work at the pub any more. She's dead.

* * *

Finn and Purcell drive me to Sydney, where Uncle Jack meets me in his Ford Fairlane with the price still on it. I sleep in the back seat all the way to Albury. Uncle Jack's car turns into the back yard, I leap out of the car and run up the back stairs three at a time and into Dad's big bearhug. We cling to each other. Much time passes. We squeeze hard. There are no tears, no tears at all. We mount the steps into the upstairs flat where Katherine Ann, John, Peter and The Hood watch television in disbelief.

I'll Take You
Home Kathleen

'Kathleen Isobel Waterstreet, 42, was found dead in her bed by her husband, well-known local publican William (Bill).' The *Border Morning Mail* story, short, blunt and brutally to the point, destroys what little hope remained that we're all just having a bad dream. She died suddenly of an apparent heart attack and is survived by Dad and us.

The mouth on the Indonesian woman in the painting above the fireplace seems to grimace. Traffic slows down to a crawl in Smollett Street out of respect, and the bar is closed for the funeral. Brady's pub across the road makes plenty this day. Suits are found for everyone except The Hood. Dad wants him to go although he's only eight. He'll always remember.

The Black Mass at St Pat's is something Mum would have been proud of if she wasn't lying in the teak casket with silver handles on the sides and an intricate Jesus Christ on the lid. The coffin is in the middle of the aisle on top of a collapsible gurney. Nana Waterstreet sings and I don't cry. Aunt Mary sings as beautifully as she does over 2CO beamed all over Australia by the magic of regional radio. I don't cry.

As advertised in the funeral notice in the *Border* classified section, the cortege leaves St Patrick's church and makes its way to the new Roman Catholic portion of the Albury cemetery. Living quarters were cramped at the cemetery so the authorities purchased the block of houses across the road, knocked them down and divided the block into Protestant, Catholic and others. Unlike the crumbling headstones and broken arches and dewinged angels of the old cemetery, the new cemetery is fully seeded with sturdy buffalo grass and all headstones above grass level are banned. Every body will have a foot square brass plaque set in the ground. The idea is to create the feeling and atmosphere of a golf course without bunkers. Holy but efficient.

Mum's plaque isn't ready but Adams Brothers Funeral Directors have sheets of artificial turf neatly laid like bath mats around the hole in the ground. They back the hearse over and the casket rests on two planks as we surround her and hold each other's hands. Ashes to ashes. Earth to earth. Four of Adams' boys hold the white straps stiff as the planks are gently removed. Mum's coffin—without the silver Jesus Christ on a cross, which has been unscrewed and given to Dad to keep as a souvenir—is let down hand over hand like an 18-gallon keg into the cellar. One of the boys loses his grip near the bottom and Mum's casket falls loudly on one side. We look in and the lid has held. Nothing had ever gone right for Mum in her whole life. I do burst out crying after all. The clods bury Mum side on, a shovel at a time.

* * *

We recover at Poppa Monahan's in Townsend Street for the wake. The barmen set up a temporary bar on crates with a linen sheet. There are all types of sherry for starters and whisky, Scottish and Australian, to kick things along. But Mum's wake has none of the cheer and merriment of Grandpa Monahan's five years earlier. Then, the songs and the sausages and the sauce never ended. Now, people arrive and leave quickly, despite the free booze. No one feels like singing at first. The men stand together in cigarette smoke on the verandah. The women sit in the kitchen and lounge room. All speak in whispers. Poppa has just lost her second child and nurses her large glass of sherry in the folds of her dress between her knees.

An aunt comes over to me and says that it's all right for me as I've only known Mum for sixteen years whereas she has known her all her life.

The only voices raised are those screaming to shut the fly screen verandah door as the mozzies and the flies are plaguing Albury this summer. The women keep their hats on as a mark of respect. Mrs Westie has made and quartered meat sandwiches which nobody touches and will have to make do for lunches tomorrow. A personal fly spray has come onto the market shelves this summer and people pass it to each other after doing their own extremities and behind their ears. It keeps the mozzies off but flies seem to love it and stick on you even if you flick your hand quickly.

Sadness gives way to melancholy and melancholy gives way to melody, and we sing I'll Take You Home Again Kathleen like a hymn, real slow, on the verandah brushing flies off each other. Everyone somehow knows the words and the women join the men and we sing it over and over and over again without ever smiling. The singing is always the high point after the funeral. But this is different. At Grandpa Monahan's we sang all sorts of songs, even Rudolph the Red-nosed Reindeer although it was August. Now you'd swear you were in a church the singing is so slow, but there isn't a dry eye or nose on Poppa's verandah. Hankies come out like a magicians' convention.

Dad gets us all in the car and we drive the block home and into the back yard. Dad opens the back bar for the boarders. They need it.

The phone rings off the hook with calls from all over the place. Georgina wishes she'd been there. I say she was, in a way: I was thinking of her all the time. She seems more upset than me but Greeks are like that.

They take everything personally. I miss you and yes of course I love you. More than ever.

She's enrolling in arts at Sydney University. We'll be together forever. She speaks to Dad, which somehow cheers him up. I don't know what she said but Dad is smiling as he passes the black saloon bar phone back to me. It has a big mouthpiece like an ice cream scoop and you can hear as clear as a bell. You'd swear it's a local call.

I'm making my mind up slowly, I say, but I'm going off the life of medicine and think I might do law. Georgina is pleased as she intends to do law herself after arts. She's a natural. Nobody can ever beat her in an argument.

I can smell her through the phone. These big Bakelite handsets are phenomenal.

I hop behind the bar and help Dad. Work takes our minds off Mum lying side on in her hole in the Roman Catholic portion. The soil will be settling down around her.

Ten Minute
Warning

The *Border Morning Mail* may have the franchise
on the funeral notices but only the *Sydney Morning
Herald* publishes the leaving certificate results. In alphabetical order, and typeset so small that Dad reaches for
the glass bottom of an old lemonade bottle he uses for
crosswords. It's understood Mum would have been
chuffed with the results and seventh place in the state
in Physics with Honours in Chemistry and four A's.
Dad tears out the results and puts them in his Daily
Missal by his bed. I go back to Kings Newsagency to
fetch another copy of the *Herald* but We've sold out
he says with a wink.

Georgina got the *Herald* at dawn in Sydney but
didn't want to spoil anything by breaking the news by
phone. Bundles of *Heralds* arrive on the first Viscount
at Albury Aerodrome for local readers interested in

news beyond wool prices and Lennox Walker's long-range weather forecast. Georgina seems to be mourning Ronald Ryan's hanging more than my Mum's death but is longing to see me again. I tell her I want to see more of her nod nod wink wink. Hard to convey on the phone.

It's definitely to be law for me at Sydney Uni. Mum didn't seem to gain much from medicine. Simmo, Grantie and The Bike have given university the flick and only Roger Ng is pursuing what he calls a turk-tree education. Knowing the lack of security in local mail delivery, Dad sends me to Sydney to do the actual enrolment weeks before uni is due to start. I ask if he has any cases coming up in court where I might do some on-the-job training at Harry Flood's side. The Flying Squad are leaving us alone and they all turned up in the back yard with the bootlids up for their Christmas bonuses, so, Charlie Boy, the heat's off for now. Just do your best.

* * *

Georgina meets me at Central Country Trains in a white dress and a flower in her hair. She jumps up and down on the spot as the Spirit of Progress slowly hiccups into the platform. Everyone in my carriage is gobsmacked and drooling visibly through the train windows as she bounces as if in slow motion on an invisible trampoline, her breasts reaching above her head as she descends and then hitting the bottom of their descent and heading skywards again like supersuperballs. Men and women alike are enthralled. All the activity of getting the luggage stops instantly and we watch the window like a large television screen. Eventually, wives kick their husbands' shins and the wet dream is over.

I rush out with Dad's largest suitcase full of clothes, a wooden tennis racquet in a vice, sheets, towels, underwear for all seasons, intending to stay only one or two nights. We missed Mum's input into the packing. I cover Georgina in kisses before reaching her mouth. Missed you. Missed you two, looking at her milky-white chest like an ocean in motion. I put the bag in a locker at the station and we catch a bus up Parramatta Road to Sydney University. The bus makes her breasts jiggle as if they're jelly and I try my very best to keep them in place.

The Admissions Office is impossible to find. It's part of the admission test, like your marks in the leaving. Step one the leaving. Step two find Admissions Office. Step three fill out a thousand-page application and enrolment form. The good news is that the Commonwealth Scholarship payments have been backdated to January the first, which means an enormous first cheque covering three months. The bad news is that it's in the mail to Albury. Dad might see it as a return on his investment. He's an old hand at forging pension cheques for boarders.

We stand in line for hours, growing intensely horny

then lapsing into slight comas in the heat. Finally I reach the admissions desk for law. A surly woman with windswept reading glasses on a chain examines my application form looking for loopholes. She sees my results and checks me out, up and down, as if I'm a fraud. Georgina, as luck would have it, gives me credibility. If she isn't at my side she's at least up to my waist.

Mr Waterstreet, I'm afraid that you are ineligible to enrol in law. Why? Is it Dad? He was framed. No, Mr Waterstreet, you have to be eighteen years of age to enrol in law.

I'm half in awe of being called Mr Waterstreet and half in mourning for being rejected and half—hang on, I think I'm out of halves. I can't repeat the leaving again. It's finished.

Mr Waterstreet—I half puff my chest out—you'll have to do something else. What's going? Agricultural science. Yuk. Veterinary science. Hate pets except racehorses. Arts. Okay, it's a deal. And then can I do law after I'm eighteen? Yes, Mr Waterstreet, you do two years arts and then first year law and then you get an arts degree at the finish of first year law. Sounds good to me.

I enrol in English, history, political science and finally physics which is the same as the Honours course in the leaving. Don't want to get addicted to work. Georgina says there's little chance of that.

We rush out of the Admissions Office and onto the

front lawns of the university where we grab each other tight and hiss and kiss and roll down the gently sloping gardens oblivious to the bindii and bees. We're uni students, in love, on heat and really really itchy. We make love in a room rented by the half-day at the People's Palace. I think of Mum and tell Georgina the story of Speech Night. She weeps more than me. You'd think it was her mother. Greeks feel everyone's pain and cry for the rest of us.

I put the flower back into her hair but on the other side where legend has it non-virgins wear it. I am so in lust that I could have made love for minutes but such concentration is beyond me and even the strongest Stay Hard cream. In between times we engage in oral sex which we firmly believe we have just invented. In a way it's even better than the real thing.

I left Albury to get a degree at university and I'm returning with the opportunity to do two degrees. Arts and law. I wear the badge Georgina pins on me at Central Station all the way to Goulburn, where I put it in my pocket. Too many people are staring at my lapel which reads Fuck LBJ.

* * *

Freshers at St John's College are treated by older students with the derision and disrespect we deserve. Part of Orientation Week involves getting dumped in Darks Forest near Wollongong completely nude and having to make your way back to college at midnight without any money. You've got no pockets to put it in anyway. Thumbing a lift with one hand over your willie is easier for some. A kindly boy scout master is unlikely to be driving along Darks Forest Road after midnight. Many Hills hoists in the area are raided and groups of freshers arrive back during the morning with tall stories and short trousers.

I win a trophy for drinking a yard-long glass of beer in record time. When I tell Dad that I've won a trophy emblazoned with my name and the year for the Annual Boat Race he says he didn't even know I could row. I explain what it is and he puts it down to years of guzzling lemonade behind the bar.

St John's College faces a twenty-storey building called the Queen Mary Nurses Home. A thousand or so nurses live there and work at the Royal Prince Alfred Hospital next to the campus. Nurses are game for Johnsmen who quickly write off the Santa Sabina Catholic girls next door as too nunpecked and closeted for fun. A vital part of a fresher's duty is to train a telescope on the side of the Queen Mary Nurses Home and move from window to window at night to catch the shift coming off or on changing clothes.

The side of the Queen Mary is divided like the game of Battleship. The top row of rooms is made up of the letters A to J. The floors are numbered 1 to 20. The fresher on nightly duty, by hourly rotation to keep the eyes crisp and sharp, is to call to his offsider to fetch the older students, usually in last year of medicine or engineering, if he makes a sighting of a nurse beginning to undress. Nurses engage in extraordinary breast enhancement exercises in the privacy of Room C12 or D8 or F17, not suspecting eye-popping freshers on duty at St John's College. Nivea cream rubbings and deep breathing exercises are as regular as clockwork. Seniors ask the Queen Mary switchboard for dates according to the nurse's room number. I blush if I see C10 rushing off to work in her uniform, knowing that she faced me the night before dressed in nothing but a tampon.

A fresher's life is not a full one. Georgina is not allowed to stay overnight even if she wanted. The rector is the lecturer in philosophy and a man of the cloth. (He eventually swaps his dog collar for a polo-neck and runs off with a nun from Santa Sabina.) We look at life through a telescope. He looks at life through a periscope. Seniors really look at life through a microscope, missing out on what's going on around them except at Queen Mary's.

On St Patrick's Day the freshers are lined up at midnight with buckets of green paint and brushes. We're instructed to paint the letters PAR out of every NO PARKING sign and road sign on campus. St John's is stocked with the best Ireland could get rid of during the potato famine. We take to the paint like ducks to water. NO KING signs appear on roads, signs and placards all over. Halfway through the night two security officers come by and shout at us to halt. We drop the paint and run for our lives. I feel we're in the IRA when two shots whiz past my left shoulder on their way to the Women's College. I fall to the ground, grazing my knees and assuming the position, the foetal position. As it turns out, the security guys get into more trouble than we do. The *Australian* gives us front page and we appear meek and humble on This Day Tonight on the ABC. The college pays to remove the green paint.

I eventually find my way to the lecture halls, where I am but one of hundreds. Taking notes seems optional, which means to me no way Jose.

In the midst of early term I get a call from Dad. The pub has burned down.

* * *

When I arrive in Albury the following morning, Dad is sleeping in the back section with a few of the boarders. He'd fallen asleep with a cigarette or two in his hand on the couch after another big night. He awoke to find the lounge room alight and the Indonesian lady over the fireplace gasping for breath and looking very green. He woke my brothers and sister. John, always a late sleeper, asked for five more minutes.

We've lost everything of Mum's. I walk with Dad through the flooded and blackened front bar where men are openly weeping. Up the stairs and into the flat where all Mum's dresses, hats and fox-fur stoles are powder. The blackened silver cross from her coffin lies in the ashes. Hundreds of 33, 78 and 45 rpm records are all melted together into big black blobs of vinyl. Colin Simpson's *The Big Country* is lost and never read.

Dad had watched from the footpath with Katherine Ann, John, Peter and The Hood in pyjamas. The flames spat when they caught hold of the gases in the neon Waterstreets Hotel sign. Captain Jack Saunders (retired) had grabbed a garden hose after rising from a near dead drunk. The water came out in a faint dribble. He threw water snakes at the fire, fearing it might reach the bar. Peter looked up at Dad and thought that if anyone's tears could put out the fire then Dad's would.

A temporary bar is set up in the stables out the back, where Dad holds court with stories of his lost Van Goghs and the office safe full of hundred dollar bills and the insurance monies to come. Our past has been incinerated. School records, photo albums and Katherine Ann's dolls which had transfixed me in the closet for some time.

I thought until now that hell was being barefoot in bindii. But real hell is thinking that hope is but disappointment deferred.

Waterstreets Railway Commercial Hotel rises from the ashes. The boarders sleep under the stars for a few weeks and don't pay a penny more or less. Dad's luck returns when he finds a near perfect copy of the Green Indonesian Woman on sale at Batrouney's Auctions.

Small world.

Pens down.

PS: Repeating
the Leaving

O n the sundrenched cafeteria patio, as promised in
the Northside Clinic brochure, I meet another
patient over a weak cappuccino. The patio is a sinis-
ter risk to non-smokers like myself as it is the only
refuge for the alcoholic, the addict, the depressed, the
suicidal, the schizophrenic, the manic and other inmates
to indulge their single legitimate pleasure. It's like a
stage show with smoke machines billowing from all
sides and sudden little explosions of matches and sucked
cigarettes glowing red.

Nicole is butting her cigarettes on the saucer in a
ring around her cup. It's her second stay and she's due
to begin another round of ECT tomorrow. She doesn't
know why it works and neither, still, do the doctors.
I'll be under anaesthetic, won't feel a thing, and the
next day I'll be right as rain. It didn't work for Mum

I say. Dr Yip obviously didn't treat my foot in mouth disease. Hope is what makes hospitals work. Hopelessness is what gives them work.

Nicole asks what I'm there for. I suffer from an excessive need for nurture, I say. I don't see her again which I guess is a good sign.

I begin to feel my old self again, which means I need further treatment. I eventually leave Northside with a packet of pills and a wave from Dr Yip.

* * *

Over the years I have overheard murmurings of Mum's suicide in the lounges and kitchens of aunties and uncles. On one occasion I simply nodded as if I knew it all along. It was not something I could ask for fear of an answer.

I need to inform myself. If Dad is a presence, Mum is an absence. She is harder to find but she is there, waiting to be solved, to be resolved, to be absolved, perhaps consoled. The mystery of my mother. It has to be done. Otherwise there will be no moving on.

For the cost of a stamp I obtain Mum's complete hospital records at Kenmore. She had more than her measure of misery and melancholy. I learn that she left school at fourteen, considered becoming a nun but became a typist. She joined the Air Force during the War and was ironically working in a pharmacy at the time she married.

In the five years before her death she had been in the Mercy Hospital in Albury for three months for a suspected stroke, at a private hospital in Melbourne for three months for ECT, which she only vaguely recollected, then back to the Mercy Hospital for a miscarriage and subsequent emergency hysterectomy which she barely survived. Then she had another nervous collapse, entering Mount St Evans in Sydney for further ECT, then the Heidelbrae Hospital for alcoholics at Strathfield. I recall visiting her there and seeing canvas placards strung on the visiting room walls like circus posters. They proclaimed Twelve Steps rather than Bearded Ladies or the World's Tallest Pygmy.

This was all in addition to her Kenmore admissions.

Mum believed the biggest conflict in her life was her alcoholism vs the expected life of a practising Roman Catholic. She also had five children, lost one and practised early withdrawal to avoid pregnancy, but the Church regarded even this method as contraception and accordingly sinful. This conflict stressed her and she drank. She loathed the hotel trade but was unable to leave for financial reasons. She fought her demons in and out of bed, in the Church and at the counter. If she was too sick to go to confession she became more conflicted and missed Mass. This led to further self-loathing and resort to shandies and Chateau Tanunda brandy. She drank and held her rosary beads around the bottle. The ring around the rosary would conclude in the back of an ambulance on the way to casualty.

God and His Church are cruel mistresses to those who love them.

One time we picked her up from hospital sparkling new and beaming, smelling as clean as dry cleaning from Lawrence's. In many ways it *was* like popping her in for a dry cleaning, evaporating her wetness and ironing out the wrinkles. But there seemed no way out of this endless retreat and renewal, voluntary or involuntary admissions before returning inevitably to the scene of the crime.

Mum and Dad were caught between the devil and her pale, pale blue eyes, eyes the exact colour of Our Lady of Fatima's shawl on plaster statues in churches and schools around the world. A light sky blue that scared and unsettled you if you stared too long at them. Even now in black and white photographs. They had five children, Mum too ill to look after us, us too young to look after ourselves, and Dad too busy providing for us all. The hotel gave us a sort of home, constant nursing hired as housemaids, and an income to support sending us children away from this hellhouse to boarding schools. But a life behind bars is no place for an alcoholic. Mum told me once she dreamed of having a house and garden. But how would we survive? Dad, like his father and his grandmother, knew only the pub trade. He had completed a year each of law, dentistry and arts at the universities of Sydney and Melbourne, but there wasn't much call for these talents in Albury in the 1960s.

* * *

I decide to send a $20 cheque to the Registrar of Births Deaths and Marriages. The cheque clears and I receive a certified copy of my mother's death certificate. In old-fashioned type which often pierced the page the Cause of Death says 'Chloral hydrate poisoning, such chloral hydrate having been self-ingested but whether accidentally or not the evidence adduced does not enable me to say.' It is certified 5 July 1967 and registered as no. 196/67. Death in Albury, unlike births, seems to be an everyday occurrence. I write another cheque to the Clerk of the Courts to pay for the transcript and exhibits of the inquest into the death of Kathleen Isobel Waterstreet. My years of lawyering are not going to waste.

The transcript arrives like so many other briefs but I do not open it until I am secluded in the back of a trusted coffee-shop. The inquest was a formal hearing presided over by the coroner, Mr J. J. Russell. Stan Jackling announced his appearance for the interests of the widower, Dad. Constable John Edward Power sought leave to appear to assist the coroner. He called himself as his first witness. He questioned himself very carefully. There were no trick questions.

Constable Power had been called to the hotel residence by the deceased's husband. Mum was on her back in the bedroom on a bed with a newspaper beside her. Her body was conveyed to Albury Base Hospital for a post-mortem examination. It failed to reveal the cause of death. There were no marks on her body or any suspicious circumstances. The witness questioned himself about an alleged earlier overdose of sleeping pills and informed the coroner of Mum's nervous condition which had existed for 12–15 years. She had been released from Kenmore Hospital three weeks earlier. She was an alcoholic. Constable Power found three bottles in her drawer: Antabuse, ferrous sulphate and Saroten. She had been taking chloral hydrate but he couldn't find the bottle. He said that the stomach contents etc. of the deceased were conveyed to the government analyst in Sydney. I wince as Dad must have behind Mr Jackling.

Dad was called to give evidence of having breakfast in the bedroom at about 8 a.m. Mum did various duties around the hotel until 11 a.m. and returned to the bedroom where Dad had dozed off. She told him that he would not be needed in the bar until lunchtime. I know that they probably worked the night before until the wee small hours. Dad woke up and went to the bathroom at 12.10 p.m. He heard Mum breathing heavily in bed. That wasn't unusual as she suffered from asthma among many other things. He returned from the bathroom and Mum appeared to be dead. She had not been unduly depressed, and never mentioned any intention of taking her own life. Dad called the family doctor, Dr Twomey, who had scheduled her to Kenmore. Dad was unaware Mum had seen Dr Twomey's locum recently for a script for chloral hydrate but knew she was discharged from Kenmore on chloral hydrate.

Dr Howard Webber was the Acting Government Medical Officer and he said he performed the autopsy. He said his examination left him completely in the dark. He received the government analyst's report and was now certain that death was caused by chloral hydrate poisoning. Mr Jackling cross-examined him about the rate of absorption of the drug in the stomach. The high doses in her liver and kidneys had no relation to the amount swallowed. He guessed that it had been taken within the three hours prior to her death. Jackling pressed him to concede that an alcoholic may be more susceptible to the drug and unable to deal rapidly with it. He agreed. Jackling asked if it were possible or not for a person to die of some type of heart trouble and there to be no evidence of it in post mortem. Webber said that it was possible. However the coroner immediately questioned Webber: You have no doubt that the cause of death was from chloral hydrate poisoning? I have no doubt, he replied.

Dr Twomey was called to testify. He had attended Mum for over twelve years for chronic alcoholism and drug addiction. He spoke to her on the telephone two days before she died. She seemed very well. He said chronic alcoholism commonly produces injury to the heart. When mixed together with chloral hydrate it leads to acute collapse. No alcohol was in her body. He said small amounts of the drug can cause sudden death, especially with a history such as hers. Jackling wanted an open finding of a heart attack. The coroner asked the doctor a question. Wouldn't there be signs of such heart failure? Not necessarily, he replied. However, Mum had just been to the locum and had received a prescription for a 200 ml bottle of chloral hydrate at a dosage of 10 ml three times a day, with five repeats. On her discharge from Kenmore she was prescribed only 10 ml at night. Her death had been precipitated with a large ingestion of chloral hydrate that morning.

A county coroner gives the dead the benefit of the doubt. The dead are not present or represented at their inquest. Even suicide notes are unreliable memoirs. Mum was cold stone sober. Her recent life had been hell. She wore a caliper on her right leg from a stroke. She had been scheduled to a mental institution three times in the last year. She was an alcoholic imprisoned in a pub. She had five children to mind and was often out of her own. Taking her own life might have been a mercy killing.

The truth of the matter is there is nothing to forgive. Nothing in her life or her way of death. It's not her shame I need to overcome but my own. It fuelled me for years.

I don't believe for one minute Mum took her own life. The locum prescribed three times the measure of chloral hydrate that the hospital had discharged her on. She had been relatively happy and working. She was a conscientious Catholic to a fault. Suicide is a mortal sin, requiring one to go straight to hell without any hope of parole or purgatory.

The real evidence is staring me straight in the face. Constable Power observed her lying on her back with the newspaper beside her. No one deliberately swallows a fatal dose of poison, goes to bed and begins to read the morning newspaper before dying. Not even the *Border Morning Mail*.